Abigail's Veil:

A Domestic Violence Handbook for Clergy & Church Leaders

Min. Carolyn J. Thompson

ISBN: 0692632948

ISBN 13: 9780692632949

Cover Photo By: Marcio Martins (2007)

Scriptural verse from which Abigail's Veil was birthed:

"...and the name of his wife was Abigail; and she was a woman of good understanding and of a beautiful countenance; but the man was churlish and evil in his doings; ..."

I Samuel 25:3 (KJV)

1) Wives [only] are to submit themselves to their husbands.

2) He is the "king of his castle," and nobody has a right to tell him how to run his house, including the church.

3) God hates divorce, so it is a sin to leave him. Just continue to pray.

4) A woman's body is not her own.

Just a few traditional church myths & beliefs that cause INJURY AND/OR DEATH!

"He and I attended church together for years and everyone knew he was beating on me... even our pastor." --S. Williams

"I didn't think anyone would believe me. After all, he was the Pastor and the congregation worshipped him" - Anonymous wife of a pastor

CONTENTS

About the Author

Minister Carolyn Jennings Thompson presides as a District Court Judge in the Ninth Judicial District in the state of North Carolina. She hears various types of cases including the abuse, neglect and dependency of children, juvenile delinquency issues, the collapse of families and marriages, and numerous cases involving domestic violence. As a minister and judge, she is inspired to educate the church community regarding victims of domestic abuse. Many Christians seek pastoral care and counseling, *trusting* the advice of church leaders. In her unique role as judge and minister, Thompson has seen up close how church leaders sometimes agonize over whether to get involved in such "private" issues as domestic violence. Her dual role provides perspective of the church's legal responsibility and its biblically moral obligation not to remain silent based upon religious traditions, stigmas and myths.

Prior to becoming a judge, she advocated on behalf of domestic violence victims for over thirteen years as a domestic/family law attorney. Her exposure to domestic violence as a child and in personal relationships, she is compelled to issue a call for education on the matter within the church community. Admittedly, she too wore the *veil*, just *as* so many women in church.

In May 2007, she completed the Pastoral Care program at Duke University's Divinity School, which enables her to volunteer as a hospital chaplain. On November 4, 2008, Judge Thompson was elected as the first female judge to preside in the Ninth Judicial District in over fifteen years. Her county seat is Oxford, North Carolina, however, she holds court in nearby Vance, Warren, Franklin and Granville counties. With a Bachelor of Arts degree in sociology from Hampton University and a Juris Doctorate degree from North Carolina Central University School of Law, she is also a licensed and ordained Minister of the Gospel.

In 2008, she founded ABIGAIL'S VEIL to provide domestic violence training for clergy and church leaders. The need to inform clergy became obvious during many years of representing abused women and children. Many stayed in their abusive homes and relationships based on pastoral counseling, church traditions, and stigmas promoted as part and parcel of church doctrines. As an advocate for families living free of violence, Thompson hopes and prays that God will grant her wisdom and resources to boldly educate the faith community about preventing domestic violence.

Throughout her legal and ministerial career, Thompson has served as board member and general member to legal and community-focused organizations, including but not limited to the Granville County Human Relations Commission; Granville County Families Living Violence Free, Inc.; Granville County Judicial Attendance Council (a.k.a. Truancy Court); Granville County Juvenile Crime Prevention Council; Granville County Interdenominational Ministerial Alliance; Franklin County Domestic Violence Task Force; Warren County Domestic Violence Task Force; and the Oxford Chapter of Les Gemme, Incorporated.

Giving all honor to God, Minister Thompson is a recipient of numerous recognitions and certificates of appreciation for her community service. Most recent acknowledgments of her commitment to service include: Certificate of Specialization in Juvenile Court issued by the North Carolina Judicial Department of the Administrative Office of Courts; the 2014 Women of Justice Award for Public Service issued by the North Carolina Lawyers Weekly; and the 2015 Power of One award issued by the Women's Economic Equity Project of Henderson, North Carolina.

She is blessed to be the wife of a loving husband, First Sergeant John E. Thompson Jr. (Ret. Army), and together they are the parents of a blended family of children Arthur Jr., Aaron, Cathryn, Brittany, and John III, and grandchildren Teaghan, Marissa, and Audrey. Their family's creed is and shall remain, "I can do ALL things through Christ who is OUR strength" (Phil. 4:13).

FORWARD

This book is dedicated to my mother and father, Eunice Mayfield-Poole and James E. Jennings Jr. In 2008, my childhood dreams were realized when you both placed the judicial robe on my shoulders. I pray your untold story of struggle and "in spite of" survival will be honored in this book. Thank you for allowing my wings to expand without limits.

Dad, I am so proud to always be your "baby girl." I am so thankful for our relationship's growth over the years; your encouragement means more than I can say.

Mom, you have always been my beacon for advocating on behalf of women and children. You are my best friend and my role model. The mantle you carry has inspired me to walk out this charge called ministry.

I love you both,

Cat

A Special Thank You

To Aunt Shelia, my Editor-in-Chief (smile):

Thank you for taking the time to help me with this long overdue project. I appreciate your constructive input and wisdom. You encouraged me to finally finish what God placed in my heart. Thank you for sharing your many gifts.

PREFACE

The intent of this book is to provide clergy and those in a position of leadership within the body of the church with basic information regarding domestic violence. Serving as spiritual counselors for those suffering intimate violence, the clergy and church leadership should have necessary scriptural and statutory tools to appropriately advise others without compromising their safety.

Most of the material herein has been presented in seminar or workshop setting at numerous churches. The goals of the sessions presented herein are to:

1) cover legal and biblical responsibilities of the church regarding disclosed and suspected domestic violence within a congregation or within the scope of pastoral care
2) identify some of the signs and symptoms of abuse
3) make informed decisions about disclosed and/or suspected abuse
4) address those myths, stigmas, religious traditions, and ecclesiastical teachings that prevent the church from being a real resource for intimate violence victims
5) understand the terms and conditions of legal (civil) restraining orders and what the church can do when the abuser and the victim attend the same church.

SCOPE OF SEMINAR MATERIAL

➢ The seminar includes an overview of legal and scriptural references to domestic violence. The laws referenced herein are based upon the North Carolina General Statutes (2015) only.

➢ Given that statistics show that 95 percent of domestic violence victims are women and their children, the seminar is limited to acts of intimate violence against women and their children women.[1] The gender-specific references are not intended to ignore the significant number of reported and unreported male victims of abuse. Further, the information herein does not pretend that men are not abused just because of gender, size and strength. They too can suffer at the hands of a fractious mate. **Violence does not discriminate based upon race, creed, gender, age or economic status**. However, the purpose of this material is to address the heavily reported and statistically maintained data that suggest that most victims are women.

➢ The participants discuss the five case scenarios located in the workbook section. The purpose is to generate open dialogue regarding abusive behaviors and the effects on their targeted victims. The group is encouraged to compare their knowledge of scriptural principles to current legal guidelines.

➢ Church by-laws, protocol and policies are reviewed as they relate to the church's responsibility to report, respond and recognize when abusers are in key positions within the organization.

THE FINE PRINT: *The seminar material and this handbook are designed to provide authoritative information in regard to the subject matter covered. The author and information provided are not to be considered as legal, psychological, or other professional services. If legal advice or other expert assistance is required, the services of a competent and licensed professional should be sought.*

---

[1] U.S. Department of Justice, Office on Violence Against Women (OVW), 145 N Street, NE, Suite 10W.121. Washington, D.C. 20530, 202-307-6026. Or see http://www.justice.gov/ovw

Chapter 1: Abigail's Story

A. The Woman

In Chapter 25 of I Samuel, there is a woman described to the reader only by her countenance and character. The Scripture describes her as "…the woman was intelligent and beautiful in appearance." It is the part about her "appearance" that captured my spirit as God began to minister to me as I conceived *Abigail's Veil.* An air of assurance, beauty and good church-like etiquette was her VEIL.

Throughout I Samuel 25, there are signs of emotional and financial abuse by Abigail's husband. Her husband's description alludes to domestic violence and an unhealthy relationship. Ná bal is described as churlish, which means rude, mean, brutal, and harsh.[2] In addition, he is described as "evil in all his doing" and the son of Belial which means he was an unbeliever. Ná bal epitomized the typical abuser who controls all of the household assets. But it would appear that Abigail kept her VEIL on, so to speak, to hide the abuse, just as many women in the church today do as well.

When we find Abigail in I Samuel, it is because the author has given us heads up that her husband, Ná bal, is an evil man, churlish in all his ways. Right away, the author points out the dichotomy that exists in this couple's household. She is portrayed as being respected as a woman of wisdom and good character. He on the other hand, is portrayed as a fool with a reputation for being mean and evil. In today's church, she would likely represent the typical married woman seeking a relationship with God and praying for the day the seat next to her will hold her husband. Or

---

[2] *Webster's Dictionary.*

you can recognize Abigail in our churches seated next to her abuser, wearing a veil that hides her fear, her shame and her hopelessness. However, based upon her outward appearance, one might never know about the silent suffering.

In the text, we find David's men encamped around Ná bal's land and possessions. David sent young messengers to Ná bal requesting just a little sustenance to help feed his army. The message to Ná bal included a reminder that while his army of six hundred men surrounded the land, at no time was anything ever taken. In fact, David's men acted as a shield protecting Ná bal and his "stuff."

Ná bal no doubt knew of David's presence and was well aware of the unmerited protection being provided to him. But in spite of this, Na´bal was disrespectful to David, in the style of a churlish person. He asked David's messengers, "Who is this David, son of Jesse?" and "Why should I help feed him and his troops when as far as I know, he could be a runaway slave?" By now, this insult was intentional because one simply could not exist in the land without knowing the great warrior and future king, David.

Once David heard of this insulting man's response, he was so incensed that he told four hundred of his six-hundred-strong battalion to gird up with their swords for one man. David was hot! In all of his anger, David personally prepared to make Ná bal an offer he could not refuse. He planned to wipe out Ná bal and all that he owned in response to this grave insult - Abigail lived with Ná bal so this included her and all that she loved too.

In the Bible, when the word "But" appears, we know to pause because God is about to shift the winds. The atmosphere of imminent harm was about to meet a sacrifice of intercession by Abigail. Sure enough, in verse 14, it reads in part "But one of the young men told Abigail, Ná bal's wife…" There was something about her character—the way she was known to handle Ná bal's evil doings in the past—which made these men confide in her. Remember that the author of this Scripture took the time to tell us about her wisdom and her appearance.

The men told her about David's message and Ná bal's churlish response. They reminded her that Ná bal was "such a son of Bĕ lĭ-al that a man cannot speak to him" (verse 17). It was a case of a heart hardened to the things of God and His people. This evil man had to know that there would be wrath to follow his provocative insults. Just as Abigail would later plead her case to David, Ná bal was a fool and acted accordingly (verse 25).

As expected, Abigail went into protective mode. After all, David was coming to kill and to destroy her home and everyone in it (verse 17). She instructed the men to gather up some groceries for David and his men as a peace offering to precede her arrival. Perhaps she knew better than to personally appear at another's man feet with her abusive husband's goods. So as she instructed, the men delivered and she followed later.

This story never tells us about Abigail's religious background as it does about Na'bal's (verse 3). However, the next few verses give us some insight as she reminds David of the promises spoken over his life by God (verses 26–31). Her "as the Lord liveth" plea puts Abigail in church with us. Her religious witness and knowledge of Jewish history testify to an early training in a godly home, and acquaintance with the teachings of the prophets in Israel.[3] She represents the church lady unequally yoked with a

---

[3] Herbert Lockyer, *All the Women of the Bible* (Grand Rapids, Michigan: Zondervan, 1967).

nonbeliever yet she holds on to her faith. Abigail even uses the meaning of the man's name to convince David that his wrath would be a waste of time. After all, she is married to a fool, "for as his name is, so is he—Ná bal."

Through these verses, the vision of "Abigail's Veil" bubbled up, providing the inspiration for this book and a catalyst for outreach ministry in this area of great need. Abigail represented the modern-day abused woman who takes the blow for her kids and her family. Look at her plea to David after she bowed herself to the ground. "Upon me, my lord, upon me let this iniquity be:" was Abigail's attempt to step into the path of a blow to her household (verse 24). In violent homes with children and other defenseless persons, the victim will often step in to take the hit to protect them. Upon her the abuse will continue but not to her babies.

Eventually, you can just feel David's temper subsiding as he listens to Abigail reminding him of his great battles and victories, battles that were ordained by God. She tells him not to spoil the legacy by shedding blood unnecessarily, out of vengeance (verse 31). David returned to his senses and blessed God for sending Abigail to him just in time to stop a slaughter. He also spoke a blessing over her for her discretion and advice. Indeed, "she was a woman of good understanding" (verse 3).

David took the groceries and sent her home with a promise not to harm her nor her home. But when Abigail returned home, Ná bal was having a liquor-house party like a king. The same man who could not spare a few crumbs for David and his men who protected all that he owned found enough money to have a house party. Ná bal was drunk as a fish when she came through the door. Like a lot of victims of domestic abuse, she knew that trying to talk with him while he was intoxicated was not the prudent. This was not the time to tell Ná bal that she took groceries out of *his* house to another man, especially to David.

Pause here. I want to emphasize a point that will be explained further in this book. Alcohol abuse and other addictions are not causes of domestic violence. Such compulsions just make the circumstances worse and the abuser will use his inebriation as an excuse. The abuser's already violent tendencies have been given more fuel to do more harm by way of badly impaired judgment. Abigail must have known from prior incidents of his churlish and evil behaviors not to talk to him when he was drunk. So she said nothing until the next morning (verse 36).

Somebody say, "But joy comes in the morning!" Amen! The next morning, when Ná bal was sober, Abigail told him about everything including how she saved the house from destruction with a bag of groceries and kindness to David. As a result of what he heard, Ná bal had a heart attack and died on the spot. In sum, she killed him with her kindness.

Now when David, oh pretty-boy David, who loved women, heard that Ná bal was dead he sent his servants back to Abigail's house (formerly Ná bal's home) to bring her to him. Ten days later, David "communed" with her and took her as his new wife (formerly Ná bal's wife verse 3).

God will deliver and restore!

B. The Veil

In this passage from I Samuel 25, the accounting of Abigail's life under Ná bal's rule does not suggest a veil explicitly. By outward appearance, she seemed as if everything was perfect in her home. But the veil was there, given the likelihood of domestic violence. There are two sides to every veil. Underneath the veil, Abigail hid the truth about home's hell; she used the outside of her veil to keep out other people's prying eyes. She wore a veil of secrecy to protect her private pain. Women like Abigail choose to put up a shield because so many in the church are not ready to hear their real testimony. The people she should be able to trust with her secret pain at the altar—the church leadership—are uninformed about the realities of domestic abuse.

On the outside she had everything: a wealthy husband who owned a bountiful harvest, wisdom that people respected, and beauty. The opinion of the public would have begged the question, "What does she have to complain about?" This is a primary stigma embedded into the veil that weighs down so many women. Even the sheerest veil feels unbearably heavy for the strongest faith-filled woman who feels trapped by the church's traditional opinions, shame and misplaced blame, myths born out of misinterpretations of Scripture, and expectations that she should "stay and pray" or "cleave and believe" so that he will change with her prayers.

The fact that the author of I Samuel took the time to describe Abigail suggests that her appearance had a lot to do with how others viewed her. According to this passage, she was a woman of wisdom and beauty *in appearance*. But she lived with a foolish man who was known to be evil in all of his doings. Her public face in times of trouble is probably what the frightened messengers remembered when they quickly tracked her down after Ná bal's insult. There was something about this woman who lived in a wrecked marriage but never let on that she was living in such conditions. Her *countenance* was the veil that helped to birth this **Abigail's Veil ministry**. The same countenance that exists today in many abused women attending church.

So often, we attend church with the need to appear as though everything is all right. I challenge you to count the number of times you are asked, "How are you this Sunday morning, sister?" Instinctively, in all of our spirituality, we answer with one of the following: "Oh, I'm just fine," "I'm blessed and highly favored," or "God is good all the time." You know the rest. All the while we are hurting under a veil of pretense in our religiously correct responses.

I use the example of the church lady with an intact outward appearance during the Abigail workshops. The audience can usually identify with the woman coming to church with perfectly applied Mary Kay makeup, Berkshire stockings, big hat tilted to one side and the latest first-lady outfit to match. This is the veil she wears to cover the story underneath. She wears a veil of secrecy to protect her private pain. It is better for her to put up a front because the church is not ready to hear her real testimony. The church is not ready to respond to her cry for help from an abusive relationship. If she tells her story, just as it is, the church that is not informed about domestic violence will create another veil for her. The veil keeps her pain and shame covered because of religious stigmas and tradition's bondage.

Abigail's Veil deals with the woman underneath the veil of secrecy, shame, and pain. An informed church is an empowered church when it comes to dealing with violence - from the pulpit to the church's front doors. Notice that I started from the leadership in the pulpit; that is directly because of my experiences representing pastors', trustees' and deacons' wives.

In my humble opinion, a pastor's wife, - a.k.a., First-Lady – wears one of the heaviest of all veils in the church. There is tremendous pressure to look the part and play the part despite the difficulty at home with an abusive husband who happens to be the pastor. In appearance, she is the role model for the other ladies in the church. After all she sits up front so that all can see her. When no one else says, "Amen" to his off-base sermons, it is her duty to set the atmosphere of praise. They are an impenetrable team.

I am reminded of a conversation with a former pastor's wife after an Abigail's Veil workshop. I saw her tears fall during the workshop, but did not know the depth of her pain until we spoke. She told me some horror stories of being held hostage by his abuse and impossible expectations in the church. She was the pastor's wife and "he was worshipped" by the parishioners. Under the *veil*, she endured five years of repeated rape, drug abuse, rumored infidelity with church members, beatings, and threats to leave her penniless. But on the outside of the *veil*, they were the perfect couple who lived the prosperity ministry that he preached. She kept their secrets until one night of rage brought her to death's door. She said, "I knew that on that Saturday night I was supposed to die and he would get away with it. I just remember grabbing the keys and running. I never looked back." The conversation ended when she said agitatedly, "He preached the very next day as if nothing happened. And do you know that to this day, a lot of the church members believe his story that I left him for no reason? Now, he's playing the victim!"

I have presided over numerous cases involving domestic violence. Those that stand out include sincere pleadings from victims wanting to dismiss their cases or to set aside the court's order of protection because of their pastor's advice. According to some of these women, they want to remove the restraining order so the abuser can participate in marital counseling without the threat of arrest. Somehow, they have been convinced that the abuse is a marital issue which holds the victim equally responsible. Right then, there is a warning signal flashing in my spirit of discernment. There is no such thing as marital counseling in an abusive relationship. The two are very different and never combine the two. In marital counseling, the victim undertakes a VEIL of *shared* responsibility for their marital problems. Domestic violence in a marriage or any relationship is beyond discord and there is only one person responsible for the abuse – the abuser. Besides, there is no amount of discord that can ever justify abuse. So, I cringe at the notion of pastoral counseling to dismiss a victim's court ordered protection without further information regarding abuser treatment and individual counseling for the abused person.

Chapter 2 : What Makes Domestic Violence Domestic and Violent?

I. Defining Domestic Violence

A. The Nutshell Law

In North Carolina, the laws define domestic violence as one or more of the acts upon an aggrieved party (hereafter *victim*) or upon a minor child living with or in the custody of the victim. The abuser must currently have or have had a personal relationship with the victim. Self-defense is not included as one of those acts. In summary, the "acts" referred to include:

(1) Attempting to cause bodily injury, or intentionally causing bodily injury; or

(2) Placing the victim or a member of the victim's family or household in fear of imminent serious bodily injury or continued harassment that rises to such a level as to inflict substantial emotional distress; or

(3) Committing any sexual act defined by another statute (G.S. 14-27.2 – 27.7)

A key element in defining the unhealthy and unsafe tie between the parties is that there must have been a PERSONAL relationship between them. The law goes on to describe and provide examples of qualifying relationships covered by this law:

(1) Are current or former spouses;

(2) Are persons of the opposite sex who live together or have lived together;

(3) Are related as parents and children. This includes someone acting in a parent's capacity and authority (in loco parentis) to a minor child. Grandparents and grandchildren are included also. However, an Order of Protection against children is limited to over the age of 16.

(4) Are persons who have a child in common;

(5) Are current or former household members; or

(6) Are persons of the opposite sex who are in a dating relationship or have been in a dating relationship. This is more than a casual "hook-up" or ordinary fraternization in a business or social context. [4]

The trend of advocacy groups and organizations encourages the reclassification of domestic relationships to a more inclusive term, Intimate Partner. Intimate partner violence (IPV) is a serious, preventable public health problem that affects millions of Americans. The term "intimate partner violence" describes physical, sexual, or psychological harm by a current or former partner or spouse. This type of violence can occur among heterosexual or same-sex couples and does not require sexual intimacy.[5]

B. Anger and Addiction Are No Defense

Nowhere in the law is there an exception for the abuser's addictions or use of some impairing substance. Nor is there an exception for an abuser with anger management issues. Use of impairing substances such as alcohol during the act of violence does not negate the violence any

---

[4] Definition of domestic violence, North Carolina General Statute Section 50B-1 (2015).
[5] Centers for Disease Control and Prevention.
http://www.cdc.gov/violenceprevention/intimatepartnerviolence/index.html

more than being angry. In many cases the alcohol is just the mechanism used by an abuser who already intends to commit an act of violence. In sum, it is an excuse, not an explanation. The same for those claiming that anger "made" them do it. If anger were the cause of the abuser's acts of violence, how is it that he does not abuse his boss or people in general? Anger is one of the abuser's tools used to inflict power and control over the victim. The abuser is in need of addiction recovery treatment and anger management classes for sure. But more importantly, an abuser treatment program has to be successfully completed before the violence can end.

C.   Legal Protection – Two Courts, Two Approaches

In the North Carolina, specifically in my judicial district, the victim has two options for relief. One is through civil court and the other is through criminal court. This may sound protective but it is really burdensome for the traumatized victim whose every movement was previously controlled by a routine of violence and financial neglect. The difficulty for the victim is that she is required to appear multiple times in order to receive relief. Complainants who receive Emergency/Ex Parte Domestic Violence Protection Orders (DVPO) are frequently frustrated by the requirement to return to the courthouse repeatedly for civil and criminal sessions of courts. Consider this scenario:

Day 1 – (Civil Court): Plaintiff/Victim arrives for Ex Parte Order after last night's beating; she is required to return another day because the Defendant needs to be served with the petition and the Ex Parte DVPO before the Court can hear evidence to support a one-year DVPO. If she fails to come back for the evidentiary hearing, the Court can dismiss her entire case or allow the emergency order to expire. She's told to return to Civil Court next week.

Day 2 – (Criminal Court): Defendant arrested for Assault on a Female charge for the *same* incident; Plaintiff/Victim is now the State's witness and must appear or the case will be dismissed; bond is set for the abuser by the court but another date for trial is set, requiring her to come again.

Day 3 – (Civil Court): Next week comes, but the Defendant has not been served with the victim's Civil Summons and Complaint and the case is continued again in order to find the Defendant for service. After years of unemployment at the demand of the abuser, she finally obtains a new job to support the kids.

Day 4 – (Criminal Court): It's now time for trial but the Defendant's recently appointed attorney needs a continuance for defense preparation. The Plaintiff/Victim took off last week for Civil Court and her new boss has threatened to fire her. Meanwhile, the Defendant is out on bond and is determined to convince the victim to drop the charges and the DVPO.

And so on, and so on …

Can you feel the frustration of the victim and how she may feel like giving up? This scenario does not even address the typical situations of those without reliable transportation, childcare arrangements or witnesses who cannot continue coming back to court. Such obstacles are exacerbated by the number of required visits to the courthouse. Unfortunately, there are a lot of court systems that are not equipped to address victims' civil and criminal complaints about the SAME incident of abuse on the SAME day of court. Moreover, every time the victim leaves her undisclosed shelter or other safe haven in order to appear in court, she is exposed to more violence by her abuser.

If you are providing pastoral care for the victim who is preparing to go through the rigors of court appearances, try to brace her for the redundancy. Minimize the fear and frustration by supporting her through each court encounter. If you are not able to personally appear with the victim in court, leave her in the capable hands of the local domestic violence advocacy organization.

Just as a brief overview, see below some of the distinctions regarding the two courts:

CRIMINAL   vs.   **CIVIL**

CRIMINAL	CIVIL
PARTIES ARE STATE vs. DEFENDANT	PARTIES ARE PLAINTIFF vs. DEFENDANT
THE ABUSED IS THE COMPLAINANT WITNESS FOR THE STATE	THE ABUSED IS THE ONLY PROPONENT OF WHAT HAPPENED
DEFENDANT IS SERVED W/A WARRANT FOR CRIMINAL CHARGES	DEFENDANT IS SERVED W/ALLEGATIONS SWORN TO BY THE ABUSED
IN N.C., THE DEFENDANT IS HELD FOR 48 HOURS FOR DOMESTIC ASSAULT BEFORE HE CAN APPEAR BEFORE JUDGE	THE DEFENDANT IS SERVED WITH A PROTECTIVE ORDER AND GIVEN UP TO 10 DAYS TO RESPOND BEFORE A JUDGE
STATE HAS AUTHORITY NOT TO DISMISS CASE EVEN IF VICTIM REQUESTS DISMISSAL (IT'S THE STATE'S CASE)	PLAINTIFF CAN INDEPENDENTLY FILE A VOLUNTARY DISMISSAL AND/OR CAN MOTION THE COURT TO SET ASIDE THE DVPO
CUSTODY OF THE CHILDREN NOT ADDRESSED	TEMPORARY CUSTODY OF THEIR CHILDREN CAN BE ADDRESSED IN A DVPO
DEFENDANT CAN OBTAIN COURT-APPOINTED ATTORNEY OR HIRE ATTORNEY	DEFENDANT NOT ENTITLED TO COURT-APPOINTED ATTORNEY AND NEITHER IS THE PLAINTIFF
VIOLATION OF RESTRAINING ORDER CAN RESULT IN JAIL	VIOLATION OF RESTRAINING ORDER CAN RESULT IN JAIL

II. Some Types of Abuse

A. Economic

Notice how Ná bal controlled the house, including the financial matters of the house. In this situation, the abuser controls all of the household funds and hers. I have represented women who are not allowed to work outside of the home. This kept them in total dependency on the abuser for the basic necessities. There are those who have no clue about how to use a debit card or checkbook because the abuser controls every aspect of the finances.

After an Abigail's Veil workshop a few years ago, a young woman with a baby on her hip whispered to me that she needed to speak with me. We quietly exited the room and huddled in a dark corner outside the church. She told me about her mate's control of her disability check and all monies for food. According to her, she was convinced to leave her family miles away and had not seen them in years because of him. She wanted to return home because she was afraid of him eventually extending the physical abuse to their baby girl. She received a type of disability check in addition to WIC each month but the abuser kept all of that from her. This young lady did not even know her own social security number.

This is just one of many examples of financial abuse. It keeps the abused isolated and in fear of homelessness. When women attempt to think about leaving under these circumstances, the fear of not knowing how to survive without the abuser solidifies his control. Try to imagine the anxiety of trying to find a job after seclusion from the world. It is difficult to make ends meet when you do not have a clue about those ends in the first place.

Working outside the home is usually a sign of independence, a risk of exposure, or a possibility of escape. So it makes sense to the abuser to forbid it. If the abuser allows his victim to work, you better know that she is under pressure to return home promptly. She is careful not to socialize for fear of being falsely accused of infidelity. Employment may not last long for the abused because of missed days. The abuser who intentionally beats the facial area or bruises the dominant hand knows that the victim cannot show up for work. Data suggest that victims lose a total of almost eight million days of paid work— the equivalent of more than 32,000 full-time jobs and women raped by an intimate partner (21.5 percent) lost an average of 8.1 days from paid work.[6]

B. Sexual

Even as between spouses, No means No! It's true that the *Holy Bible* notes that spouses' bodies are not their own, and that spouses should come together for intimacy to keep the enemy from exposing them to temptation (1 Corinthians 7:4-5). However, the same aforementioned verse refers to a couple honoring the one, true living God with the sacrifice of self. In verse 3 of the same passage, the Lord issues a charge for the "husband to render unto the wife due benevolence." There is nothing godly about raping and sexually assaulting anyone, especially your life mate or spouse. Despite the myth, rape can occur even in marriages, not just in unwed relationships.

---

[6] National Center for Injury Prevention and Control. Costs of Intimate Partner Violence Against Women in the United States. Atlanta (GA): Centers for Disease Control and Prevention; 2003.Available at http://www.cdc.gov/ncipc/pub-res/ipv_cost/IPVBook-Final-Feb18.pdf

Let's be very clear that this type of abuse is not because the intimate partner has a head-ache tonight, and every night as a part of ongoing marital discord. Sexual abuse occurs when the batterer has a warped need to control through sexually deviant, illegal, and unwanted sexual acts. For the abuser who stayed awake in church just long enough to hear a sermon about the roles of wives, he will take away only the part that serves his abusive agenda. Upon hearing that a woman's body is not her own and her husband is the head over her, the abuser will use that against his wife. The obligation to read the entire text in its whole context is lost on the abuser. So, the abuser may choose to ignore this verse about a husband's proper role: "Likewise, ye husbands, dwell with them according to knowledge, giving honor unto the wife, as unto the weaker vessel, and as being heirs together of the grace of life; that your prayers be not hindered" (1 Pet. 3:7 KJV). The Bible's reference to words such as, "likewise husbands," falls on deaf ears of the abuser.

C. Emotional

It is possible to commit acts of violence against a victim without ever coming into physical contact. Repeated intimidation and threats of physical injury can make a victim believe she is in imminent danger. An abuser that punches walls and slams objects sends a message of fear.

Living in a constant state of fear is just one aspect of emotional abuse. Victims' experiences of emotional abuse are subjective, but exist just as much, as physical injuries. A barrage of degrading remarks can cause damage to a person's state of mind. Without the benefit of a cast, stitches, makeup or vanishing cream, a victim is forced to suffer an injury within her very essence, deep beneath the already broken self-esteem.

As an aside, in my days of providing legal counsel to women wanting to get out of their abusive relationships, they would tell me horrific recounts of emotional abuse. These women could easily show me the old and new physical scars but their emotional scars were the ones that left indelible marks. A recurring sentiment during these sessions was how their mates beat down their mind. They spoke of how the name calling, constant yelling, vile obscenities, and false accusations of infidelity echoed in their minds even in the absence of their mates and long after the physical scars had healed.

I will never forget how one client exclaimed, "I just wish he would just hit me already and get it over with." Tearfully she explained that at least the bruises would heal. In her assessment, a blow to her body was less of an assault. She had been enduring years of constant reminders that she was "nothing but a fat, ugly whore" and how "nobody's gonna want you" if she were to leave him. She began to believe him deep in her being, so when she looked into a mirror she saw the lie that her spirit man had been repeatedly fed. In this situation, time does not heal all wounds.

Emotional battering leaves the victim internally disfigured. The emotionally battered woman can no longer recognize herself or entertain independent thoughts. Her wits have been jumbled into a mass of incomplete thoughts; her laughter has been hampered by fear; her ability to concentrate on small tasks has been impaired; and now, she second-guesses her ability to complete the most basic of self-maintenance projects. She has become a mere shell of her former self.

According to North Carolina statutes, substantial emotional distress has to be proven. Without a testimony supported by concrete evidence, the courts can find it difficult to make "Findings of Fact" about emotional abuse. The courts look for evidence of a pattern of abuse, behavior that has caused emotional harm. Thus the burden of proof is on the victim. I have listened to women struggle to find words significant enough to express the damage caused by the constant name calling, reminders of how worthless she is to this world. If you have ever experienced how degradation, humiliation, and fear-driven isolation emotionally disrupts your peace of mind, it is something you can readily recognize during your pastoral counseling.

Emotional abuse is more than a complaint that the victim feels bad or that there is marital discord. But it is difficult for a lay person to explain for the purpose of obtaining legal relief that is more than, "he hurt my feelings." Arguably, North Carolina's statutory reference to "substantial" suggests that the complainant has to lay a foundation of borderline mental illness or an emotional defect that requires psychological help. Certainly, documentation from a mental health physician helps the court assess the need for a protective order but it not the only source of evidence. In fact, I am a hesitant to even defer to the psychologists' diagnosis for the purpose of issuing an order. Deferring to such a diagnosis feeds the myth that all women who stay in abusive relationships are mentally ill. We should not lend our ears to this argument because it causes insensitivity in a culture already too quick to criticize victims. The notion that victims are mentally ill makes it easier for the uninformed to say, "Oh, she must be crazy to stay in that situation." Dismissing victims as nutty is just too easy, even if one can thereby get better sleep in the short term, having been released from any further responsibility on the issue of domestic violence.

Constantly hearing abasing remarks about one's worth, appearance, and intellect wears down the mind's defenses. Before long, the mind begins to agree with the abuser. Only a spiritual deliverance will lift the hidden scars from the soul. Such scars are hard to describe to a judge in an attempt to get a restraining order. The insensitive and untrained listener will make excuses for the abuser and attempt to convince the victim that it is all in her mind.

Emotionally scarred victims have a heightened sensitivity to another's tone of voice. Someone raises his voice and causes her heart to speed up due to nervous energy. The victim who lived for years with the yelling mate cannot deal with loud voices. The memories are just too fresh.

There may be a vacancy in their eyes when you attempt to counsel the emotionally abused parishioners. It is most difficult for them to make eye contact perhaps because of the VEIL. When the woman tries to make excuses for her abuser, she will often refer to his behavior only timidly.

D. Physical

The most commonly discussed abuse is physical abuse. When I preside over a case involving physical abuse, the absence of injury may create confusion for the average person. However, the abuser does not need to leave marks and bruises for the abuse to be classified as physical. For example, shoving and pushing do not necessarily result in physical injuries but they are types of physical abuse nonetheless. When one abuser held his victim down on a couch while he slowly dripped his saliva onto her face, he accomplished his intent of exerting power and control. During this hearing, I saw the victim's eyes relive the moment of feeling helpless, not just because he tied her hands or because his weight prevented her movement but because she could feel his cold spit running down to her hairline into her eardrum. In this case, the abuser purposely and slowly spat on her face while repeatedly asking, "what-cha gonna do about it?" No amount of surgery in the natural realm can heal that injury.

In this free and most powerful country in the world, statistics reveal Americans' staggering inability to eliminate and prevent domestic violence. For example,[7]:

- Every 9 seconds in the US a woman is assaulted or beaten.
- Domestic violence is the leading cause of injury to women – more than car accidents, muggings, and rapes combined.
- Domestic violence victims lose nearly 8 million days of paid work per year in the US - the equivalent of 32,000 full-time jobs.
- Every day in the US, more than three women are murdered by their husbands or boyfriends.

[7] See http://domesticviolencestatistics.org/domestic-violence-statistics, accessed Oct. 8, 2015

- The costs of intimate partner violence in the US alone exceed $5.8 billion per year: $4.1 billion are for direct medical and health care services, while productivity losses account for nearly $1.8 billion.
- Studies suggest that up to 10 million children witness some form of domestic violence annually.

III. Domestic Violence Causes Collateral Damage

The relationship between the victim and abuser affects the entire family unit, the concerned friends, the neighbors and even the local community. The abuse may occur behind closed doors but the impact can be felt beyond those doors.

The mother who repeatedly asked her daughter, "Is everything ok?" or "Is he hurting you?" regrets the call that something really bad has happened. The mother immediately criticizes her inquiries as inadequate. I have talked to mothers of victims who said that they knew something was wrong but could not get beyond the repeated denials and rejections of help. They feel helpless and lost when their mother's intuition screams like a siren. They feel the conflict between being intrusive in their daughters' personal affairs and the urge to protect them.

This dilemma heightens when there are grandchildren caught in the middle. During visits, their grandchildren show signs of trauma or monitored conversations. Grandparents feel constrained by unspoken boundary lines. They don't want to make their children feel threatened by potential removal of their grandchildren; and they don't want to stand by while their grandchildren suffer direct and indirect harm.

As an attorney, my advice to grandmothers and mothers of abused women focused on empowering them to act. I had to get them beyond the uncomfortable decision to step on toes, possibly offend the son-in-law, and even strain familial ties. A frank discussion about the alternative had to be on the table during these consultations. That required playing out the scenario of the long term effects on grandchildren who were constantly exposed to domestic violence; or the call that their daughter was in the hospital or worse, the morgue; or the "what if you do nothing and say nothing" scenario. Preparing grandparents to file custody suits for their grandchildren were some of the most difficult cases. I had to remind them that it was not about hurting their children but about protecting their grandchildren. Not every situation required such drastic action. Sometimes, only advising them to make an anonymous call to the local child welfare agency for a wellness check or to make a wellness check request by the local police or sheriff's department proved adequate. The point here is to do something, or say something in response to those suspicions. You may save a life or prevent further injury.

I had an opportunity to talk with the sister of a victim murdered by her abuser. She recalled all the efforts made to help protect her sister from the tragic end. Before her death, the family took turns checking on her sister by phone or random home visits. The ex-husband became determined to terrorize the victim regardless of family members' efforts to intervene. Just days before her murder, the victim shared with her sister that her living in fear and in hiding had to stop. She wanted her independence back and was determined to take back her independence. The victim's abuser followed her to an ATM and shot her in the head.

At the candlelight vigil with hundreds of mourners, the community expressed its frustration and determination to stomp out domestic violence. But the eyes of the victim's mother told a story of unspeakable loss and damage. The victim's sister spoke to the crowd as the family's spokesperson vowing never to let this death fade in everyone's call to action against domestic violence. At this moment of community solidarity, I saw police officers' tears as they remembered responding to the fatal call. I heard countless memories of the victim's friends, co-workers, and church members of how vibrant she lived before domestic violence held her hostage. Even the local domestic violence advocacy agency representatives were there taking in the loss as if their own sister had been killed by violence.

We cannot forget to mention that the abuser's family is also affected by his violence. For example, the abuser's family members may feel that same sense of helplessness. I spoke with a mother of an abuser after an Abigail's Veil workshop. She was the pastor's wife and felt compelled to tell me in a quiet corner of the church that her son was abusing his girlfriend. She tried to talk to him about it but feared for her own safety because of his known outbursts, especially when he was noncompliant with medication. She told me about how the girlfriend's calls for help were increasing. During the last call, she could actually hear her son's ranting while throwing furniture. Without passing judgment, I suggested that she push beyond her feelings of guilt and shame if her son were arrested after calling the police. The police would arrest if they found probable cause and that would be based upon her son's behavior, not hers. We also talked about creating a safe haven for the girlfriend until she was ready to move on. We talked about the possibility of involuntary commitment of her mentally ill son who had well-documented incidents of behavior dangerous to himself and others. She too had to come into a reality check about the "what if" scenario.

Sometimes the abuser's family members feel vicariously at fault for his destructive behavior. The father of a teenager who admitted killing his 15-year-old girlfriend said this to a reporter outside the courthouse:

> "I've been knowing the [victim's] family a long time. I'm sorry," said Willie Malloy. "Ain't nothing I can say, but I'm just sorry. I'm sorry about all of this. Ain't nothing I can do. I just wish it never would have happened."[8]

Hindsight statements of this father suggested signs were there but like everyone else, they just attributed them to typical teenaged behavior. Both families suffered damages. The victim's family buried a child and the abuser's family will visit a child behind locked prison doors for several years.

---

[8] "FAMILY OF TEEN MURDER SUSPECT SPEAKS FOR THE FIRST TIME," by Nicole Carr and Greg Barnes, Fayetteville, WTVD Channel 11 ABC News, February 10, 2015

Chapter 3 : Are the Church Doors Really Open?

Judge not, that you be not judged (Mathew 7:1 KJV)

This is not the time to judge or offer criticism about her situation or her. Remember the invitation to come *as you are*. Do not offer advice about how to change the situation at this moment. This is the time to listen. The victim who finally gathered the nerve to seek a kind ear does not need to hear suggestions about her appearance, for example. Through the church's doors is a sanctuary for what the world would consider unreal and abnormal. Think about it. Where else can we go in public to jump around, dance uncontrollably, cry and slobber all over ourselves, and talk aloud to someone that is not physically present without fear of criticism - or worse, petitions for court orders involuntarily committing us? Our altar calls are like the triage rooms for the victim's pain and suffering. So do not listen with worldly ears; hear the horrific without censorship.

Watch Your Mouth, Please!

On February 24, 2014, while traveling to court, I was listening to a popular radio station known for its gospel songs and radio hosts. The female radio host, who is best known for her music and "Christian" morning show, announced that she was preparing to read what she described as a "disturbing" letter from a listener. She went on to read the woman's plea for guidance because of her abusive husband who served in a key position in the church. This modern-day Ná bal wanted her to leave *his* house and to take their baby with her. The listener wrote that she did not believe in divorce because of her church-like upbringing and just wanted the abuse to stop. When the radio host finished reading the letter, her first response to this desperate plea was, "First of all, you sound bipolar."

At this point, I could feel my skin crawling and anger rising. It did not get any better for the anonymous writer. If the letter writer was listening in shame, embarrassment, and confusion, this radio host's callousness would have put her through a form of public abuse called *re-victimization*. This gospel-song-singing "Christian" host, went on to rant about how she did not understand "these women" who complain that they are abused but do not want a divorce. She further stated how according to her review of the Bible that nowhere is divorce prohibited but that instead God hated sin. Right then I knew she was not well versed in this area. The Bible does state that God hates divorce and within that same passage it is written that God also hates violence (Mal 2:16 KJV). To add further injury, the host tried to explain away the "bipolar" radio diagnosis as stemming from the beleaguered woman's confusion by ending the session with, "You're obviously confused."

This type of callous treatment by uniformed people is what victims of abuse dread so much about disclosure. If a victim confides in an uninformed person who is in a position of ministerial authority by mere title, status and forum, it can be very delicate. If this radio personality did not have the answer, she should have simply directed the listener to the professionals. This radio personality inflicted further emotional abuse by causing the writer (and those like her who were listening) to think that it was her fault for staying; that she had some type of mental-defect for even wanting her marriage; and that her pain was not valid. The host missed a crucial opportunity to assist a victim of violence at the altar call of her radio segment.

Had she read the Scriptures carefully, she would have known that Malachi 2:16 reads in part that, "For the Lord, the God of Israel says: "I hate divorce and marital separation…" This same text also states that God also hates "…him who covers his garment [his wife] with violence. Therefore, keep watch upon your spirit, that you deal not treacherously and faithlessly." So many passages of Scripture are taken out of context by a clergy member or by those like this thoughtless singer-host, resulting in potentially bad consequences for the recipient of ill-informed advice. In this case, the singer-host did not even know, or chose to ignore, the latter portion of this Bible passage, a passage that would have yielded a better understanding of the listener's state of mind and commitment to her teachings.

All day in court I kept thinking about how terrible it was for the letter writer to hear these very negative comments, not to mention those who were also suffering from abuse and happened to be listening to the insensitive radio host's segment. Where was the love of Christ in calling this woman bi-polar? We never know how or when our advice will produce fruit and what type of fruit. So we should be careful that our pastoral comments to a victim are screened carefully by the urging of the Holy Spirit, as well as any knowledge we may have on the subject matter. If we do not know what to say, then say nothing right then or nothing at all. In other words, as clergy we should stay in our lanes and direct the person to someone who knows about the subject of intimate violence. Just because we have the mic, that it does not mean we should always speak.

Needless to say, I have made it a point never to listen to that station from 9:00 am to 10:00am.

Can You Handle the Truth?

When a pastor or preacher for the hour ends a sermon with a petition that "the doors of the church are open...," I wonder how prepared the petitioner is to receive a request for prayer due to severe abuse. It can be confusing in some churches because there might be a mistaken intent to use this moment as a call for membership candidates. Instead, this is good soil for disclosure and a plea for help from a victim. Sure, it may be a routine, but it actually could be an ideal time for helping the abused. For the abused who pressed their way to church, benediction is the worst time. They feel like they have to prepare to return home just as they came to church, abused. In this moment of safety among others, if the abused person decides a prayer request is a morsel of relief, please be prepared to help.

Do not expect the victim's disclosure to be in great detail. She may not be ready to talk about the sexual violence but may feel more comfortable saying he "makes me do things I don't want to do." This is not the time to examine her for more details at the altar. Just listen until she has finished releasing the burden of despair. You cannot fix her home in the five-minute altar call. There will be a moment of opportunity when she is ready.

If you are fortunate enough to be at the altar when a victim comes for help, know that you are called in that moment TO HELP, NOT TO JUDGE in any form. You were selected by your church leader or pastor to assist at the altar because have matured in the faith of prayers. Focus on the person's spiritual needs at that moment. She may just need to whisper it in your ear that home is a living nightmare. This could be the first step to her self-empowerment. Sometimes, it is just about being a listening ear, a sounding board for what has been silenced by fear and his control.

The primary question to ask is, *"Are you Safe Now?* Stick to this message about Safety First and it will keep you, the congregation and the traumatized family safe. Gone are the days when we can say a little prayer during our services and consider the matter done. We have to be ready in all seasons for the person who answers "No, I am not safe." The question then becomes, "can you handle the truth?" What you say and do next will and can be a barrier or a breakthrough.

Here are some examples of what **NOT TO SAY** when a victim discloses abuse:

DON'T SAY/ASK	WHY NOT
Have you two considered marital counseling?	This assumes that both have a role in the abuse and indirectly blames the victim. Marital counseling is totally different from abuser treatment and abuse counseling. Both of the aforementioned provide individual help to the couple. Marital counseling would, however, put the abused in the room right beside the abuser. This endangers the victim, as disclosure could lead to additional harm for disclosing. Therefore, you are not likely to get to truth anyway. What could she possibly say to you in his presence that will keep her safe behind closed doors?
Have you prayed about it and him?	Yes, prayer is essential. But in this moment, her safety is key. If she hasn't prayed because she doesn't have a relationship with our God, the question assigns failure to her
What did you do or say before he hit you?	There is no justifiable reason, ever, for the assault. Again, the question blames the victim.
Have you thought about how leaving will break up your children's home?	It was his decision to destroy the home with his violence. Her responsibility is to protect the children and this question places guilt on the victim for trying.
Do you think he just needs some time to cool off?	There is no such thing as a cooling-off period. This suggest that his anger/uncontrolled emotions can simply dissipate with time. This does not recognize the abuser's need for treatment.
Are you sure that this is not just some type of misunderstanding?	This devalues an already difficult subject to discuss. Given that the victim was courageous enough to say,

	"Enough is Enough," her injuries and abuse should be validated. This abuse is real.
But Rob is such a good guy, a solid Christian in this church	*Continued on next page* You have just joined "team abuse" and sent a message of condonation. Re-victimization has occurred because somehow she has become the villain for tarnishing Brother Rob's reputation.
How many times has this happened? Or Why did you go back? Or Why did you stay?	Let her volunteer whether the abuse has previously occurred and to what degree she was injured. These questions that if this is a one-time incident, it is not as severe as she puts it. Reasons for going back or staying will vary from victim to victim. These questions, at this moment of vulnerability, suggest that there is something wrong with her mind and/or her. With appropriate counseling, she will come to understand the need to remove herself from harm's way. But you cannot tell her to leave. It has to come from her.
"Girl, if I were you …"; or "If a man hit me like that, he'd draw back a nub"; or "Why didn't you hit back?"; or "You must be crazy to stay with a man like that."	These statements and questions, reinforce the abuser's emotional damage. They make her feel weak, mentally ill, and/or inferior to other women. You are a pillar of strength but she needs you to be one that is supportive.

+

Chapter 4 : Why Does She Stay?

There's no cookie cutter answer.

Recent media reporting of a sports figure punching his fiancé in an elevator swarmed the public for weeks. All eyes were on this young couple and public opinion focused on the issue of domestic violence as if it were some new concept. Then, the victim became the villain when she married her abuser shortly after the video. Instead of asking where the couple registered for gifts, the media picked up the quest to talk about her decision to still marry him. She became a bad role model for every woman in a relationship. There were accusations that her motives to marry had to do with her fiancé's huge sports contract. For about an additional two weeks, some networks ran a commercial campaign centered on abused women explaining, "Why I Stayed." While, the circus turned away from the need to address the abuser, the better approach would have been to ask, "Why does the abuser abuse?"

Fear of the Unknown

Feelings of having no place to go are very prevalent, especially in cases of financial abuse. The abuser who controls the household purse strings, as Ná bal did, does not permit his victim to have a world beyond his fingertips. Staying with the devil she knows is more concrete than facing the unknown world without the means to survive. Control via isolation serves its purpose because the victim often feels it is impossible to make it without him; that she cannot possibly call friends and relatives after all this time of isolation from their presence; or that an escape would only be temporary because he would likely find her quickly.

Fear of Criticism and Condemnation

For the socially visible and conscientious victim, expectations of others hold the keys to her escape. Be it real or imagined, the victim in this case feels a great deal of responsibility to uphold a certain image. For example, I represented a pastor's wife who repeatedly expressed concerns about how her leaving would affect the church. During the initial consultation, she said her leaving would "split the church." Never mind her bruised eye still had not healed and her attempt to cover it with makeup only made it look worse. The fear of condemnation by the church and the church community is real, just as real as the fear of having to face her abuser daily. For a lot of "first ladies" this role is their life, their sole identity. At the end of our meeting, I escorted her to the back parking lot of my office. She purposely parked there to avoid explaining to her abusive pastoring husband that a member mentioned seeing her car at my office. Needless to say, she closed her file with my office and never pursued further legal help – until a few years later when she had her *"enough is enough"* moment.

No Place to Hide

The victim has the burden of trying to figure out a place of temporary safety until a permanent place can be secured. If she has lived under the foot of his isolation, threats to harm her and/or her family, and financial control, then she may feel unable to find independent shelter. He knows everybody she knows and everywhere she is likely to seek shelter. The abuser uses social media and tracking devices to monitor her movement and communication with others. He will not have any hesitation to even follow her to the church, daycare where kids attend, relatives' homes and friends' home.

No Place to Go for Safety and Shelter

Unfortunately, the local domestic violence advocacy organizations have limited shelters due to inadequate funding. So many families are required to relocate outside of their local communities because the local shelters are closed or full. The impact can have a negative impact on situations we may take for granted such as, the children will have to register at another school away from friends or their very own support systems; Medicaid benefits are delayed; or lack of transportation back to the court's jurisdiction where the restraining order was filed for protection.

She Still Loves Him

Interestingly, it is not uncommon for a victim of abuse to still love her abuser. I have listened to numerous accounts of survival that end with, "I still love him." This emotion may be another factor in her decision to stay. I would wager the average spouse or intimate partner in an abusive relationship never imagined that the person who once caressed her back, looked deeply in her eyes with promises of love and affection, and held her in his arms of protection would become her worst nightmare.

Financial Dependence on Abuser

If the abuser is the sole breadwinner and keeper of the purse strings, she will not have the means to get away and maintain daily needs without him. There are women who fully committed to the role of being submissive and totally dependent on her abuser for everything. In this type of relationship, the victim may not even know her social security number, may not have a license to drive, or may never have a clue about the household expenses. She is kept completely out of any decision regarding the household. Even for her personal hygiene needs, she has to ask her abuser for permission and money.

Chapter 5: She Can't Change Him - Love's Got Nothing to Do with It!

There is no fear in love! (1 John 4:18 KJV)

"There is no fear in love, but full-grown love turns fear out of doors and expels every trace of terror! For fear brings with it the thought of punishment, and [so] he who is afraid has not reached the full maturity of love" (1 John 4:18 Amplified Bible). This passage states that a person's love for another should not require the use of fear tactics and terrorism to control that person. On the contrary, the abuser may return to the scene of violent acts against his victim with gestures of romance, love, and affection out of some distorted concept of love. However, this verse demands that love should cast out the need to control with violence, emotional abuse, and/or financial neglect.

We are not given information about Abigail's love for Ná bal. The text, however, lets us know that his behavior never changed even in the face of death. When the men came to her in fear of David's wrath, they pointed out that he was the kind of man who would not listen. Notice how Abigail bypasses going to Ná bal after the news. No doubt she was already familiar with his pattern of behavior and needed to take action around him. After all, David was on his way to destroy her home and all that she loved. Her urgent intercession was not new.

The abuser is not able to fully receive the love he tries to control through violence. Until he accepts the true Love of Jesus and Him as his Savior, the victim's love will never be enough. Just as a spiritual deliverance is required for her emotional healing, it is also required for the abuser to stop the violence. He too needs healing from whatever triggers his need to control with violence.

Women are by instinct given to nurture. We want to cure with a kiss, heal with a hug, and love the bad feelings away. We tend to fool ourselves into believing that we can love the man so much that he will eventually change. This fallacy so often continues right up to the wedding day, when the hopeless deadline for change expires. A wise woman advised me: "Whatever you see in him before you say, 'I do' will be etched in stone after the honeymoon. So don't go trying to change him after the wedding." Yet when he does not change, we blame the insufficiency of our love just as a victim blames herself for her abuser's behavior.

The abuser must admit that there is a problem and that he is the perpetrator of the problem. After coming to this revelation, he must want and seek help. This sincere cry for help is what the victim holds on to as a possibility of change. Their love, or the absence thereof, for each other quite frankly is irrelevant if the abuser is in denial. In the infamous lyrics to Tina Turner's song, "What's love got to do with it? … What's love but a second-hand emotion?", love has nothing to do with his decision to change. Nevertheless, this false sense of hope in sufficient love toward him will keep the cycle of abuse in motion. A glimpse of what life could be if only he was not abusive comes in rare moments of apologizing during the honeymoon phase. However, without his acceptance of responsibility and repentance, his apologies, and empty promises will inevitably lead to more violence.

Domestic violence is about the abuser's power and control over his victim. There are many ways to try to have power over another person. Battering is one form of domestic or intimate partner violence. It is characterized by the pattern of actions that an individual uses to intentionally control or dominate his intimate partner. That is why the words "power and control" are in the center of the wheel. A batterer systematically uses threats, intimidation, and coercion to instill fear in his partner. These behaviors are the spokes of the wheel. Physical and sexual violence holds it all together—this violence is the rim of the wheel.[9]

[9] Home of the Duluth website explaining the wheel's purpose, http://theduluthmodel.org/training (reprinted w/permission)

The model below is a helpful resource in conceptualizing these mechanisms of violence by abusers. This is used during workshops as a key discussion to dispel the myth that anger or some other emotion is the cause of domestic violence. **POWER AND CONTROL WHEEL**[10]

---

[10] Home of the Duluth Model: Social Change to End Violence Against Women, http://www.duluth-model.org. Featuring Domestic Abuse Intervention Programs (DAIP). 202 East Superior Street, Duluth, Minnesota 55802. (218) 722-2781.

CYCLE OF VIOLENCE WHEEL [11]

The victim can feel the shifts in the abuser's behavior before the hitting begins. Once the honeymoon phase ends the tension in the home increases. Then, aggravation and aggression toward the victim sends signals of imminent harm. This will continue as a cycle of leaving and returning for some victims, until she determines that *enough is enough*, or until she is injured - critically or fatally.

Violent Outbreak Phase

Abuser explodes, there is a major destructive act against the victim. This act could be emotional or physical.

Victim may blame herself, may fight back, may try to escape

Honeymoon Phase

Abuser pursues the victim, promises to change, send flowers, cards, letters, says he can't live without her, is charming and manipulative.

Victim wants to believe he will change, sees a glimpse of the man she fell in love with.

Tension Building Phase

Abuser is edgy, not speaking, slamming doors, breaking things, etc. Could be agitated and picking on everything.

Victim is walking on eggshells. Tries to keep the peace.

---

[11] Taken from the Eastern Refuge Society.
http://www.easternrefugesociety.org.nz/assets/uploads/2013/09/cycle-of-violence-2.jpg

It's OK to forgive him ... but from a distance!

As clergy, we will need to discuss the topic of forgiveness in some point of counseling a victim. Unforgiveness gives the offender unmerited space in our emotions and time. In T.D. Jakes's book, *Let it Go*, he wrote: *"Forgiveness, then, is a gift you must find a way to give yourself regardless of who or what has dropped you into this grievous state of affairs."[12]* The victim of abuse will not be able to completely heal if the subject of forgiveness is not properly addressed. Forgiveness does not mean what happened gives the offender an escape from responsibility and consequences. Instead, forgiveness is for the victim's benefit, providing deliverance from the cycle of abuse. The emphasis here has to be that it is alright to forgive, but that the forgiveness must be allowed to take place from a distance. Remember, Safety Is First!

Forgiveness strengthens the abused. It is a moment of empowerment for the abused NOT for the abuser. Without forgiveness, hatred, resentment, or anger takes up emotional space that is necessary for moving on as a survivor. The energy used to hold on tight to what happened and wanting the person to pay is wasted energy. It may sound hokey to some but we know it is scriptural. For God is a defender of righteousness, and He will avenge all wrongs done to His children. He will repay (Romans 12:19 KJV). Unforgiveness is a behavior born out of memories of the abuse. Despite the adage, "I can forgive but I cannot forget," there has to be an informed decision to forgive because it involves

---

[12] T. D. Jakes, *Let It Go: Forgive So You Can Be Forgiven* (New York: Atria Paperback, 2012), p. 33.

making a choice to put the memories to rest. Sure, it may take time but it is necessary before the victim can change her call-sign to SURVIVOR.

The victim does not need to confront the abuser with her forgiveness. It is an inner peace, a validation that can be achieved from a distance. Releasing herself from guilt, shame, anger, and the emotional damage caused by the abuser breaks the cycle of violence and the abuser's power and control. When the victim is able to exhale in the confidence of regaining self-control, the control shifts without input from the abuser. As clergy or as a church leader, just be there for reinforcement through counseling and prayer.

Do not enter the pastoral care sessions with the forgiveness agenda. Yes, she will have to reach that point of forgiveness so that she too can be forgiveness. Yes, forgiveness is a crucial part of healing. But the timing has to be appropriate so as not to leave an impression of condonation. She may not be ready to receive the message of forgiveness when she is still wearing the scars inside and out.

If the parties are married, this is not the opportunity to offer marital counseling with your newly found forgiveness. Remember, marital counseling is totally different from abuser treatment and domestic violence counseling for the victim. Do not put the two in a room together! Allow her declaration of forgiveness from a distance.

Chapter 6: "Pray and Stay" or "Don't Cleave, Leave" – Advising the
  Abused

"Pray and Stay"

If the church leaders have not properly studied verses about
strained marriages or apply only partial verses to marital roles, then they
can unknowingly give some misleading advice. An abused wife tends to
yield to the voice of authority from the pulpit just as she would to her
mate. If her mate attends the same church services, he will hear only the
bit that tends to justify a man's control. From the same sermon based
upon partial verses or misapplication of verses, she will hear confirmation
of her submission to his violence and he will feel validated about his
behavior. For example, the incomplete message of "only you must submit
woman" approach comes from a misapplication of Scripture.

Ephesians 5:22-23 reads: "Wives, be subject to (be submissive and
adapt yourselves) your own husbands as [a service] to the Lord. For the
husband is head of the wife as Christ is the Head of the church, Himself
being the Savior of [His] body (NASB).[13] This is where the conversation
or the message from the pulpit tends to stop. It tickles the ear of the
abuser but entraps the victim in an already emotional cage. In order to
understand the abuser's role, one has to continue reading and preaching
the following verses.

Ephesians 5:25-30 reads: "Husbands, love your wives, as Christ
loved the church and gave Himself up for her; So that He might sanctify
her, having cleansed her by the washing of water with the Word; That He
might present the church to Himself in glorious splendor, without spot or
wrinkle or any such things [that she might be holy and faultless]. **Even so**

---

[13] The Ryrie NASB Study Bible: A Complete Study and Reference Tool, Charles Caldwell Ryrie, Th.D., Ph.D., Moody Publishers, Chicago (1995 Update).

husbands should love their wives as [being in a sense] their own bodies. He who loves his own wife loves himself. For no man ever hated his own flesh, but nourishes and carefully protects and cherishes it, as Christ does the church" (NASB).

Where in the follow-up verses [or any verse in the Bible] does it allow for brutal beatings, verbal battering or abusive control? Instead, the Scripture clearly draws a metaphor between the husband-wife relationship and the Christ-church relationship. The charge here to nourish, protect and cherish is forgotten or intentionally excluded from the mind of the abuser. Shamefully, it is not preached as much as the concurrent charge to the wife.

If you dare advise the victim to stay and pray because her prayers will change him, remember that prayer is a conversation.[14] Please advise her to listen for the response according to the will of God and for church expectations. So if the answer or response from Holy Spirit is that she should leave the abuser, do not try to insert your own personal and traditional beliefs. It is imperative that you pray for wisdom and understanding. Unless the Prince of Peace - our Lord and Savior who declared that the greatest gift is LOVE, clearly directs you tell her, "stay" then DO NOT advise her to cleave.

Telling the abused to stay out of an obligation to family togetherness is wrong. The decision to leave for safety and emotional wellbeing does not break up the home. Rather, it is the abuser's decision to use violence and abusive behaviors that destroys the family. Those

---

[14] Rev. Rick Warren. As quoted during an October 2015 Domestic Violence Training Conference for Clergy with Min. Carolyn Thompson and sponsored by Safe Space, Inc., Louisburg, NC.

living with an abusive man are not living in a safe haven, but rather in a den of fear.

Paul's instruction in 1 Corinthians 7:10 (KJV) starts with a disclaimer that it is not his charge but the Lord's to instruct married people to stay. In this passage, the unbelieving husband has the covering of his holy wife. However, an unbelieving husband has to want and to actually participate in the sanctification process. He cannot hide behind his wife's salvation while continuing to abuse her. By definition, if he is without Christian faith, how will he know to become humble and turn from his evil ways? Is there going to be an epiphany during a barrage of blows to her head that he should change because she takes it like a good Christian? He might go to his grave in disbelief just as Nábal and never realize the intercessory prayers of his wife. Nevertheless, a biblically committed wife believing in the abiding power of her prayers will endure the abuse based upon the narrow interpretation of these verses. Instead, you may consider explaining to her that while God hates divorce, he also hates him who covers his garment [his wife] with violence (Malachi 2:16 AMP). Further, that her husband has already "put away" the marriage by dealing treacherously against her with acts of violence. She should also be directed to the final catch-all disclaimer in the same passage by Paul: "...but God has called us to peace" (1 Corinthians 7:15 KJV). There is no peace in a marriage clothed in violence.

"Don't Cleave, Leave"

It should not be surprising to know that a lot of the victims of abuse love their mates. Do not assume that divorce is the ultimate goal for the victim. Some do not want to end the relationship but simply want the violence to end. They are still able to remember the yesterday when he was loving, caring and romantic. In some instances, he is still the man that she wants to spend the rest of her life trying to change. Unfortunately, she could lose her life in the process of trying to change him. This notion is an example of the "cleave and believe" phase of the domestic violence cycle.

However, do not automatically jump to an escape plan either. Securing and maintaining her safety is paramount in every disclosure of abuse. Separation and/or divorce discussions may be a deal breaker if you should bring them up as an option. For the devoutly committed spouse, divorce is not an option. She does not want a divorce but simply wants the abuse to stop. She wants to bring back those loving feelings that have been lost by some defect in their marriage.

Respectfully, do not allow our pastoral need to *fix* others to take over here. It is a mistake to immediately go into taking control over the situation. Your coming up with ways of escape and protection without her input is just reinforcing the pre-existing POWER AND CONTROL model that she has lived under with her abuser. The only difference is that you are not controlling her with brutality. She has to be at a point where she can play an integral role in the planning and preparing for her escape. This is when you ask, "How can I help you?" or "Is there anything you need from the church?" or "What do you need?" Now, the victim is the initiator in her own deliverance and safety action plan.

The proposed safety plan may take some time to work out, especially if she is still in the home and not prepared to leave right away. The safety plan for leaving should be executed with all care and thoughtfulness because most domestic violence homicides occur during the victim's attempt to leave. **The most dangerous time for a woman who is being abused is when she tries to leave**. (See the United States Department of Justice, National Crime Victim Survey, 1995).

When I was an attorney representing victims in need of a safety plan, I often advised them to be a private investigator in their own home as they prepared to leave. Each case is different, obviously but in general there are key pieces of survival documents needed to survive beyond the abuser's control. For example, she should locate the bank account information without disturbing its location. She should write down the checking account's numbers or take the last page of its deposit slip, putting in her bra until able to safely stash it. Never keep the information in the house. This is where an enlisted trustworthy church leader or friend can help by keeping the information until the victim is ready to leave.

Another important piece of information (especially for victims leaving with children) is the abuser's social security number. The victim should know the abuser's social security number better than her own. Every child support enforcement agency will be able to track down banking, employment, and income information via a database with a social security number. The court can order that the whereabouts of the complainant not be disclosed by the child abuse enforcement agency due to the existence of domestic violence.

At all times, the victim must treat the safety plan with all possible caution. If the abuser prematurely discovers the safety plan, the victim could suffer more harm, if not death. All safety plans, including the ones mentioned herein, have to be carried out with all care and consideration of the tight control that has existed up to date. Here's a sample of things to consider when comprising a safety plan with the victim's input:

- Transportation:

    1) Do you know how to drive? If not, can we help you identify a trusted driver? Or help with a flight or bus tickets?
    2) Do you have a driver's license?
    3) Do you have access to the car keys?

- Money to Pay Bills:

    1) If there is no access to cash or accounts, is there an emergency fund offered by the church?
    2) Are there family members who can provide temporary help?

- Housing:

    1) Where are the local shelters for domestic violence victims?
    2) Does the court's protective order restrain the abuser from being in the house?
    3) Does the church have the means to provide temporary shelter, even if it means covering room and board at a local hotel?
    4) Do you know of someone with a spare room?

- Child Care:

    1) Make sure the victim requests temporary custody as part of the court's protective order.
    2) Did you share a copy of the order with the kids' daycare provider/school principal?
    3) Does the local Department of Health and Human Services have funds to help pay for child care?

Continued on next page

- Clothing:

  1) Can you take enough clothes out of the house without it being noticeable?
  2) Check into the church's clothes pantry.
  3) Secure a site for a hidden suitcase, so you can collect clothes until ready for leaving.

- Food:

  1) Are you able to slowly and carefully stow away nonperishable food until it is time to leave?
  2) Until you are able to find employment, gather information needed to qualify for food stamps and/or WIC.

- Safe, supportive person:

  1) Identify a family member and/or friend you can trust.
  2) Honestly tell them about their role and why.
  3) Connect her with a pastoral care counselor from the church and codes for imminent help (i.e. "pizza" can mean *call the police for me*).

- Communication:

  1) Obtain a disposable phone or check with the local domestic violence advocacy's office about getting a phone donation.
  2) Establish a code-word that lets others know you are being abused or that abuse is imminent, and that help is needed right away.

Rejection of You and Returning to Him ...

Statistics show that a victim of abuse is likely to return to her abuser at least eight times before making a final decision to leave. When a victim comes to court for a protection order, the number of prior dismissals should not matter. Absent a clear showing of frivolous prosecution, the courts should treat each petition as a new request for protection. I am reminded of how some of the court clerks brought files to the bench with sticky notes. On these notes, the clerk had listed the number of times the plaintiff filed domestic violence petitions that were later dismissed by the plaintiff and/or dismissed by the court for her failure to appear. The accounting of previous dismissals presumably was intended to influence my decision in some way. But after ignoring the notes or writing "So what?" a few times, I finally shared this statistic with the clerk. Needless to say, I no longer get those notes.

After helping in a rescue, do not expect to be their savior and to be given recognition or praise. The victim may try to avoid you for the next few services but don't take it personally. This may be her way of keeping a safe distance because the same woman who recently needed your urgent help has probably returned to her abusive mate. It will take a strong prompting of the Holy Spirit for the helper from becoming confused, angry or offended...I know, I know. It will not make logical sense to the average person. I know, I know. But that is where you as a pastoral counselor or trusted leader have to remember that it is not about you. This person still needs help and will probably reach out to you or someone else in the near future. The question you must answer before becoming involved and taking on the role as a pastoral care leader in this situation is, "Can you handle the possibility of the victim's return?"

Chapter 7: Confidentiality

Confidentiality - An Overview

The importance of confidentiality cannot be emphasized enough. A victim's disclosure comes with a great risk that the abuser could find out. If you are in a position of leadership and a victim comes to you, treat the disclosure with the utmost privacy and confidence. A betrayal of confidence at this point could bring harm to the victim and shut down any future opportunity to help. By law, such confidence and discretion covers any information disclosed about themselves or another for the purpose of seeking spiritual counsel and advice relative to and growing out of the information so imparted.[15]

A. Legally Protected Status of Ordained Ministers vs. Other Church Leaders (NC Law)

There are certain legal responsibilities and protections for those who provide pastoral care for the abused. The law in North Carolina describes such care as a privilege protected by the courts. In this state, an ordained minister holds a legally protected status as opposed to a church elder or other member of the five-fold ministry. For this reason, church clergy should hold an ordained status if assigned to handle pastoral care for marital problems and abusive relationships. Disclosures understandably are never so tight and neat. Do not turn away a victim just because you are not ordained. Just keep in mind that there is an expectation of trust and privacy inherent in your communications, primarily because of your leadership position.

---

[15] N.C.G.S. § 8-53.2. **Communications between clergymen and communicants**

C. Stay Off the Hell-O-Phone, This Is Not the Time for Corporate Prayer

This is not the time to get on the "hell-o-phone" to call other folks into corporate prayer about what the victim disclosed to you. You know how some of us "good" Christians act when we just have to share "the good news" with a fellow member. Picking up that phone and pretending to call others in the name of Christian help can quickly turn to hurt and gossip of that victim's affairs. It is hard enough for a victim to reach out for help, without the added fear that someone might gossip about her situation after altar call. The worst thing you can do in your quest to help is to breach that confidential relationship. One cannot imagine the horror and embarrassment of a victim who walks into whispers or abruptly ended conversations about her. Now, she has deal with stigmas from the church body even more. Not to mention, irresponsible gossip could easily lead to her abuser finding out … all in the name of so-called *help* (not Jesus).

D. What's Said at the Altar Stays at the Altar (seeking advice & comfort is   protected information).

Unless the person gives you permission to share her private information, you should never discuss it with anyone else. There is a great risk of exposing the victim to further danger should your leak get back to the abuser who may be in the same church.

The need to understand your role as a clergy, other church leader, or assigned confidant in an assumed position of authority could never be more important. Your actions and words affect the victim as well as the church you are representing. If there is a breach of confidence, you not only expose the victim to further abuse but you expose your church to legal sanctions. This is where the saying, "to whom much is given, much is required" is actually enforced by laws.

The church grapevine does not release you to talk about it. Just because it seems like everybody knows already, you are not permitted to discuss the disclosure made to you. If the victim starts talking about it with others and including that they consulted with you about the same, you are still under a duty not to disclose information.

E. The Law and Its Limits

In North Carolina, clergy hold a legally protected status. What is shared behind the curtain, at the altar or in pastoral care sessions, for example, can never be brought out in any legal action. Just the same, in many cases courts hold those entrusted with confidential information accountable.

In North Carolina, communications between clergymen and communicants are covered under North Carolina General Statute Section 8-53.2 which provides:

> No priest, rabbi, accredited Christian Science practitioner, or a clergyman or ordained minister of an established church shall be competent to testify in any action, suit or proceeding concerning any information which was communicated to him and entrusted to him in his professional capacity, and necessary to enable him to discharge the functions of his office according to the usual course of his practice or discipline, wherein such person so communicating such information about himself or another is seeking spiritual counsel and advice relative to and growing out of the information so imparted, provided, however, that this section shall not apply where communicant in open court waives the privilege conferred. (1959, c. 646; 1963, c. 200; 1967, c. 794.)

This statute is crucial to a victim wishing to tell her pastor what is really happening in her home, behind closed doors. What she shares in confidence for the purpose of obtaining your counsel cannot be used against her later in court. Only the victim can waive this privilege. It does not matter that the situation discussed has become common knowledge - as her confidant your lips are sealed. The discussion was intended as confidential at the time of your consult and that is how it should remain.

There are some requirements of this privilege protection such as 1) the person must be seeking counsel and advice of her minister and 2) the information must be entrusted to the minister as a confidential communication. State v. Andrews, 131 N.C. App 370, 507 S.E.2d 305 (1998). To err on the side of caution, let us not get caught up in the exact language of the victim when the discussion begins. She may not say to you verbatim, "This conversation is intended for the confidential purpose of seeking consultation." Protect yourself and her by assuming (yes, I said it) that the disclosure is confidential.

In criminal matters, our courts have held that there is a distinction between the status of an elder in the church and an ordained minister. In State v. Pulley, the Court held that the clergy-communication privilege does not apply to statements a [person] made in the presence of a church elder who was not an ordained minister or clergyman[16]. Quite honestly, does the average lay person crying in the arms of a praying elder know whether that elder has been ordained? It is not reasonable to expect folks coming to the altar to ask for ordination papers before pouring out their bleeding hearts. If your church leader has placed you out front with the delegated duty of providing ministerial consultation and/or pastoral care

---

[16] State v. Pulley, 180 N.C. App 54 (2006).

on behalf of the church, TAG! YOU'RE IT! Do not breach the trust of a person that comes to you for prayer and advice about her abusive situation.

F. Breaching Confidentiality Exposes the Church to Liability Actions

You may be an associate minister or an ordained elder delegated by your pastor to talk to a victim or to follow-up on their prayer request. Your pastor has given you permission to stand in his/her shoes for a specific purpose. Essentially, you have been assigned in the role of clergy or church leader while under the covering of your church. This means you may also expose your church to liability actions for breach of confidence. It doesn't matter whether you are paid or serving in a volunteer capacity - your role leads back to the church. There is an agency relationship that exists between you and the church even though it has not been put into a written document.

An agency is defined and explained as follows[17]:

A consensual relationship created by contract or by law where one party, the principal, grants authority for another party, the agent, to act on behalf of and under the control of the principal to deal with a third party. An agency relationship is fiduciary in nature, and the actions and words of an agent exchanged with a third party bind the principal.

An agreement creating an agency relationship may be express or implied, and both the agent and principal may be either an individual or an entity, such as a corporation or partnership. The principal may authorize the agent to perform a variety of tasks or may restrict the agent to specific functions, but regardless of the amount, or scope, of authority given to the agent, the agent represents the principal and is subject to the principal's control.

---

[17] http://legal-dictionary.thefreedictionary.com/agency

More important, the principal is liable for the consequences of acts that the agent has been directed to perform.

*A voluntary, <u>Good Faith</u> relationship of trust, known as a fiduciary relationship, exists between a principal [**the pastor/bishop, for example**]and an agent [**church leader/associate minister, for example**] for the benefit of the principal. This relationship requires the agent to exercise a duty of loyalty to the principal and to use reasonable care to serve and protect the interests of the principal. An agent who acts in his or her own interest violates the fiduciary duty and will be financially liable to the principal for any losses the principal incurs because of that breach of the fiduciary duty (Legal-Dictionary/The Free Dictionary.com)*

In my discussion groups, it doesn't really hit home with the participants until I paint a hypothetical of violence leading back to a breach. I give an example of the victim's husband finding out about her attempt to seek help from a church leader, Minister Smith. In turn, the church leader calls another church leader to "pray about it." Somehow, the information leaks from leader to leader until it reaches the abusive spouse who also serves as a leader in the church. He then goes home to teach his wife a lesson of about keeping their business private. The wife suffers permanent injuries after getting released from medical care. She sues for damages, alleging among other things, that she relied upon the clergy member's consultation and his promise to keep the same confidential. She further alleges that but for your breach of confidentiality, her dear sweet deacon-husband would have never injured her with his fists and feet.

Guess what? The deep pocket is not you, Minister Smith, it is the church. I end the hypothetical with the church having to pay out so much money in damages that the marquee out front has to be changed to the victim's last name (Smith's Baptist Church, for example).

Chapter 8: Let's Not Forget Lil' Abby
THE PHONE TEST - GRADE "F"

As a part of my opening during school events, I ask the students, "How many of you would accept a free smartphone from your boyfriend or girlfriend?" I go on to explain that no bill has to be paid by them for this latest iPhone because the boy/girlfriend has the phone in his/her name and will assume responsibility for the bill each month. Invariably, over half of those in the crowded gym immediately raise their hands.

The kids are asked to keep their hands lifted as I ask follow up questions such as "Would you still want the phone if you were required to check in with your friend every hour on the hour; you were not allowed to talk to anyone but him/her on this phone; if he/she maintains tabs on your texts and Internet usage (after all, they pay the bill); and your whereabouts would always be known because your "boo" pays a little more each month to place a locating app on the phone?" Slowly the hands begin to come down, but not all.

This phone test highlights how young people trying their hands at dating relationships manage to get trapped in an abusive relationship. A seemingly sweet gift can be used as a source of control. In this instance, the abuser has placed an electronic leash around his prey. Suddenly, your parents' warning that nothing in life is free makes sense. By accepting this "free" phone, the young Abigail (hereafter Abby) cannot get away from excessive texts, which she must answer promptly. A routine event such as eating dinner with the family has now become a broken pattern of endless interruptions because his/her calls must be answered or else.

Statistics reveal that nearly one in five teenage girls who have been in a relationship said a boyfriend threatened violence or self-harm if presented with a breakup.[18]

The Need to Fit In Still Exists Years Later

We can all remember the awkward feeling of the first day of school as adolescents. There was the fear of entering the cafeteria as you paraded in line, feeling that all eyes were on what you selected as the day's ensemble. Some of us may need to look back a little longer than others, but the tried and true of being an adolescent is IMAGE, IMAGE, IMAGE. What self-imposed pressure we put upon ourselves in those self-finding years. Another facet of being a teenager is having relationship savvy.

It is the popular girl's calling card to say "my boyfriend" to her squad. At some point you recognize the need to move away from the role of third wheel when you are at the mall with her and her "boo." So when the opportunity presents itself, if you are not strong enough to wait for Boaz, the first boyfriend can be the one who played on your 'awkward' moment.

During a peer session with a group of girls at a local church, a young girl explained tearfully that she did not leave her teenaged abusive boyfriend because she didn't want to feel left out with her girlfriends, all of whom had boyfriends. Schools are little towns within our towns. They have their own mayors and governing boards simply based upon popularity charts. Being connected and liked are important roles for the adolescent. Embarrassing moments come with the price of being excluded

---

[18] http://domesticviolencestatistics.org/domestic-violence-statistics/

from the daily conversation in the gossip media cloud. Imagine the weight of wanting to walk away from the most popular boyfriend because he is hitting you, but not being able to because your "friends" will take his side and ban you from the privileges afforded only to the school town's elite.

In October 2014, I listened with a mother's ear to a young girl's recollection of wanting to kill herself because it seemed easier than walking away. She sobbed throughout her testimony before a small crowd of people gathered to kick off domestic violence awareness month. I could feel her mother's heart breaking because of the unknown pain her child experienced at the hands of someone else's child. She had no clue that this seemingly innocent puppy-love moment in her daughter's life could have permanently taken her away. The girl told us how subtle the abuse began between her and the other middle-school student (yes, middle-school). The unhealthy relationship signs started with the girl altering her appearance, because he made her feel fat and ugly. By the high school years, depression had already taken her through cutting and eating disorders and she was trapped in the domestic violence cycle. Thankfully, her parents' determination to get necessary counseling exposed the violent relationship, the parents obtained a court-ordered restraining order against the boy, and she was relocated their daughter to another school.

The common denominator in this girl's recollection of adolescent domestic abuse, as so with other adolescents, is the use of cell phones and social media. I have issued a number of restraining orders for complaints of cyberbullying, harassing phone calls, and communication of threats via text messages among teens. We, the adults, do not have to feel helpless and out-of-touch. There are tools available to help us monitor this age of social media and popularity by cell phone generation. Contact your

Internet and cellular providers about apps and parental control devices. After all, We Pay The Bills!

Here are a few things to look for to see if your teens and young adults are in an abusive relationship:

- **A change in clothing style**. For example, your daughter used to be a fashion diva. Now, because he does not approve, she wears all big clothes that are clearly not her style. He does not want her wearing tight jeans because it invites attention from males. Her abuser constantly accuses her of flirting or bringing attention from other males.

- **Drastic mood swings and/or depressive countenance**. Get her to a counselor or therapist right away. She will deny any wrong doing or problems but if you know her personality and there has been an unhealthy change in behavior. Negative comments about everything and everyone.

- **Withdrawn and disappearance of old friends**. Because he demands her undivided attention constantly, she has lost all contact with her usual friends. You can find her sitting in her room when important social events, such as an important dance like the prom, are ignored.

- **Constant texts and online chatting with boyfriend**. Because of the abuser's need to control her every moment, a normal dinner will be constantly invaded by texts. She feels obligated to answer or else suffer the assaults and accusations from him. Check the phone bill. You will see scads of texts within minutes. He demands to know her whereabouts at all times.

- **Unexplained bruises and marks**. Beyond the hickie marks used to mark his territory, she will have marks and bruises hidden by layers of clothes. Pinching is popular among teenaged abusers. Listen for excuses about how he really didn't mean it or that he was just playing around.

- **Low self-esteem.** The victim cannot make eye contact, makes criticizing remarks about herself, and/or has low confidence.

- **Lower grades or has drop school activities.** The report cards will show a pattern of decline; there is no motivation to complete assignments and no interest in attending school on a regular basis. The once avid extracurricular young participant no longer wants to play sports or participate in clubs.

In North Carolina, a 15-year-old girl was killed by her 17-year-old boyfriend. The tragedy sent shock waves for months with her family remaining diligent about justice for this young girl. During an interview below with reporters, family members and their pastor recalled incidents of both teens' behaviors as hindsight red flags:

"Locklear, 15, and her then-17-year-old ex-boyfriend, Je'Michael Malloy, were in a relationship that sent up occasional red flags, mainly in Locklear's sad demeanor. It was always chalked up to puppy love problems according to family. Behavior they witnessed also sent up red flags.

Malloy's outburst at the family church involving a younger member was chalked up to a young man who just needed to cool off, said family members.

"This is not fake. This is real," said Simmons. "Je'Michael got so upset with one of the kids, and we're talking 6 or 7 years old, that he pulled

a knife."

Fisher, the church's pastor, described pulling Malloy aside to calm him down.

"We just thought 'upset, teenage boy,' but now it [we know] it was something," she said. Holding a picture of the couple headed to a winter dance at Locklear's South View High School almost puts the family in a daze.

"Je'Michael and Danielle, looking very sweet, very innocent," said Simmons. "Now looking at that photograph, you never would have though. You never would have thought. So things are not always what they seem."

In the days leading up to Locklear's murder, her family members said she was noticeably down. Locklear and Malloy, an aspiring Marine, had broken up, but again, on the surface it seemed typical of what teens go through.

"She had a deep sadness about her," said Simmons, with other family members nodding in agreement around Locklear's grave. "When at that time, hindsight would say, we should've taken out the time and stopped and said 'Dannie, what's on your mind? I can see something's not right.'"

Locklear would go missing and be killed on the same day -- March 11, 2014. However, her body was not discovered for another three weeks. Endless days of searching and speculation ended when authorities said Malloy confessed to killing his ex-girlfriend.

"For the very person who she trusted, and felt loved and cared about her, took her life," said Simmons. "That's why it's very important for the young men and women out there who are going through domestic violence [to know] it's not okay."

Locklear's friend and fellow Cape Fear High School classmate Dominic Lock would be charged in connection with helping Malloy discard Locklear's body. The 18-year-old posted a $100,000 bond shortly after he was arrested.[19]

This is an example of the opening quiz given during my session with youth groups. As an additional icebreaker, the teens openly discuss their answers which are not always as expected.

- QUIZ -

1. If your boyfriend/girlfriend offered you a free cell phone, would you accept this as a gift?

   Answer: _____

   Explain:

2. Your "boo" friend does not let you hand around your friends anymore because he/she thinks you spend too much time with them. He/She is jealous and wants you all to himself/herself. Do you stop hanging with friends? What do you say to your friends about the request?

   Answer: _____

   Explain:

3. Your boy/girlfriend wants you to text all day regardless of family, friends and your own social life. Do you think this is because he/she cares so much about you? Do you comply?

   Answer: _____

   Explain:

---

[19] "ONE YEAR LATER: DANIELLE LOCKLEAR'S FAMILY REMEMBERS SLAIN TEEN," by Nicole Carr, WTVD-11 ABC News, March 9,2015

4. He/she gets really mad at you for talking to other people even if they are your friends. He/she is always accusing you of cheating with other people. Does this mean your "boo" just loves you so much? Do you think this is just cute jealousy because they love you that much?

   Answer: _____

   Explain:

5. It is not rape if you have already had sex with your "boo" and now he/she still makes you have sex even after you said "NO."

   True _____ or False _____?

6. You said something or did something to make your boy/girlfriend mad. So you caused him/her to hit you.

   True _____ or False _____?

7. You are too young to get a restraining order against your boy/girlfriend who is also just a teenager.

   True _____ or False _____?

8. The pictures you texted your boy/girlfriend are private selfies of you naked and they promised to delete them after looking at them. Is this a crime? If he sent to another friend who posted them on some type of social media, which of them is in trouble with the law? Does deleting the pictures mean that there are gone forever?

   Explain:

9. Does pinching and pushing count as abuse? What about name calling that makes you feel dirty and/or depressed all the time?

   Explain:

10. Are your parents, caretakers, school counselors or church leaders good resources for help?

    Explain:

Chapter 9: Seven Things the Church Can Do to Help

1. <u>Start the Conversation</u>

When Jesus met the woman at the well, He did not start in on her about her sins. There was no condemnation at the well that day. He opened the door for deliverance by having a conversation. He must of have known that pouncing on her with judgment would push her away. Seven sentences by Jesus put it all on the table for her confession and immediate salvation from a life of jumping from bed to bed. He was patient but persistent until the unnamed woman confessed that He was Lord. And it was all because He started a conversation.

Domestic violence is not a comfortable subject to bring up in any forum. But protecting comfort levels protects the abuser's reign. The church can no longer hide behind the misinformed notion that violence in the home is a "private" matter. As long as it is allowed to be a secret sin, a "private" matter in a man's castle, families will suffer with the church's blessing. There has to be a conversation to open the door for victims to begin disclosure.

The church can no longer afford to have three-point messages about domestic violence somewhere around a women's day program. The issue of domestic violence needs to be engaged with the goal of eliminating abuse. From the pulpit to the front doors there has to be consistent accountability.

At the next board meeting or conference, add to the agenda the "what if" scenario. See if your staff, your ministerial team, your security detail, your Sunday school teachers and pastors are prepared to deal with the situation presented. You can learn a lot about their personal views and commitment to the protection of the church members from just talking.

I remember an attempt to self-invite Abigail's Veil to a pastor a few years ago. He proudly responded, "Oh, we don't have that issue in our church." As expected, a few weeks later, I received a call to come out. You know why? Because he had a conversation with his first-lady about our brief encounter. She shared with him how certain ladies in the church were experiencing a rough time at home because of their abusive husbands. A conversation opened the doors to informing a leader and getting help for those women. It should not take a celebrity's brutality on an elevator to bring attention to this serious issue and to bring the discussion to every household. The day-to-day home riddled with domestic violence lives that elevator scene routinely without fanfare and without relief.

Be ready to take the next step after opening up the discussion. Your next step could be one of the next six (6) suggestions. But there has to be a next step. Even if your leadership team has a concrete idea of what to do when a victim comes for help, you can never go wrong by holding a refresher meeting.

2. **Get Involved**

It sounds simple. But this is the area where the myth of private business thrives in abusive relationships. If they are attending the same church or appears under the sound of your preaching voice, then the abused and the abuser are your business. You are your brother and sister's keeper (Gen. 3:9-11 AMP).

We can preach about tithing and living right, two very personal issues close to any man's heart, but still hide behind certain myths and stigmas of the carnal world. Remember, we are all one body and if one suffers, we all suffer (1 Cor.12:12-26 AMP). Sure, there are risks involved and defensive denials may come from the family, but wouldn't you like to know that you at least asked, "Are you safe" in a situation that later revealed lethal violence?

One evening when I was still in elementary-school age, my mother and step-father, were playing cards as my brother and I watched the Mickey Mouse Club show. I remember the evening vividly even now. I was so focused on the young kids wearing the lettered sweaters spelling out M-I-C-K-E-Y. Then, suddenly, a thunderous noise broke my concentration. It was the sound of "Big John" hitting my mother and her body hitting the floor.

Instinctively, I ran out of the house for help. Barefoot and screaming, I ran to the house in front of us. I will never forget the female voice yelling back at my pleas for help as I frantically banged on her door. She said, "Get away from here with that mess, don't bring that over here!" I leaped from her porch to run down the street to the other neighbors. They did not even turn the porch light on to acknowledge my presence, and they too never came to the door. Finally, next door to our home was Ms. Annie's haunted-looking house. As kids, we avoided her yard because of the horse-like dog called Jack. Putting all imagined ghost stories aside as a kid looking for help, I banged on her door and she answered right away. She pulled me in gently and said, "Come on in child, everything 'twill be all right now." As she called the police, she assured me that Momma would be all right now. She got involved when no one else would and I felt safe.

3. **Establish and Enforce Church Policy and Bylaws of Zero Tolerance**

It has to be clear to anyone accepting a position of leadership or authority that domestic violence is not tolerated by the church. The church's written bylaws should contain prohibitions and consequences should there be evidence of violations. There can be no grey area here. You cannot serve the church and terrorize your family.

Check with your insurance company about guidelines of protection from liability. Some insurance carriers will require the church to have a written policy for issues such as child abuse before providing liability insurance. The same may apply to domestic violence disclosures.

A message of intolerance to anyone accepting a position of leadership authority has to be clear - from the pulpit to the front doors of the church. There can no longer be exceptions based upon the "good guy" vetting. Do the research before you hire clergy and appoint people to key positions. Public records, criminal records and other means of background investigations are readily available today. Thanks to social media and the Internet, you can just about find anyone or anything. Yes, even check candidates' social media postings. Filling positions in the body of the church should be as rigorous a process as screening job applications is for local business owners, banks, or school divisions.

Persons in leadership roles who cannot pass the screening process themselves should be made to relinquish their positions. In some churches it is called "sitting them down." It is an insult adding further injury to the victim while the abuser is allowed to serve in the church and it's known that he subjects his family to abuse.

If a country can take a hard stand to ban a convicted abuser from stepping foot on its soil, why is it so hard for churches to take a similar stand when it comes to its parishioners? I read a newspaper article on December 6, 2015, which had the caption, "Brown cancels Down Under tour after visa troubles." At first glance, it seemed like his visa troubles were the reason for the cancellation. But the underlying "domestic violence" references pulled me in. The author wrote about how Australia denied singer Chris Brown a visa because of his criminal conviction for assaulting popstar, Rihanna, also a singer.[20]

The singer's planned tour in Australia and New Zealand was forced to cancel and refund tickets when Australia's immigration department issued a "notice of intention to consider refusal." The former Immigration Minister, Michaelia Cash, urged authorities to refuse Brown's visa on character grounds. The former minister stated, "People need to understand if you are going to commit domestic violence and then you want to travel around the world, there are going to be countries that say to you: You cannot come in because you are not of the character we expect in Australia."

Imagine the impact on statistics and convictions if everyone took the same approach of serving notice of ZERO tolerance on domestic violence. It is a challenge for churches to take a similar stand against violence under their cathedral ceilings. The church, like the former Australian immigration minister, has to enforce a character-vetting process for those who want leadership consideration, including the pastor. The deacon who beats his wife and traumatizes their children has no business serving in such an important capacity. Sit him down. The door usher who greets and welcomes the community into the house of the Lord while

---

[20] "Brown cancels Down Under Tour after visa troubles," by Nick Perry, Associated Press. Cited in The Daily Dispatch, Henderson, North Carolina, News From the Light Side, Sunday, December 6,2015

engaging in any type of domestic abuse does not the character of one safeguarding the doors to the church.

4. <u>Get to Know Your Local Resources</u>

If you don't have the manpower nor the in-house resources to help those who disclose domestic violence, direct the person to your community's local domestic violence advocacy group. Maintain in your hands-on contact list the number for the advocacy's crisis or helpline. These soldiers of domestic violence awareness are your allies. They are relieved when you call needing direction, needing help with victims, or just hoping to partner the congregation with their agency. Invite the directors or representatives of the local domestic violence advocacy group to come speak at the church. These are the few laborers and the harvest is plentiful.

5. <u>Pass the Plate</u>

This is where the eyes tend to go into the pay-her-no-mind zone during the workshop. As clergy, we can raise an offering for every need of the storehouse and the surrounding communities. It should not be so hard to put in the church's budget line a regular donation to the local domestic violence shelters or reputable advocacy agencies. Some churches have year-round building fund campaigns in pursuit of bigger sanctuaries, but there is no room for the victim in need. Often, the victims leave home wearing no more than the shoes on their feet and pajamas, with their kids in tow. Shelters tend to have a standing wish list to defray the costs associated with emergency shelter needs. The list below is taken from a combination of local shelters.

Please consider raising funds for or purchasing the following suggested items:

____ deodorant	____ soap
____ sanitary items	____ diapers
____ tooth brush & paste	____ wash cloths & towels
____ mouth wash	____ shampoo & conditioner
____ small suitcase	____ clothes
____ your old cell phone	____ gently used coats
____ sheet sets	____ blankets
____ new pillows	____ shoes
____ can goods	____ non-perishable food
____ gas/gift cards	____ cellphone minute card
____ gently used/new toys	____ washing detergent
____ toilet paper	____ paper napkins, plates & cups
____ plastic/disposable utensils	
____ new underwear	

Even if the church is not financially able to provide monthly support to a local agency, individual efforts can go a long way. Each of us can contribute something. Consider it a personal challenge to include a shelter or advocacy program into the budget line. Sacrifice the cost of a new pair of shoes that look like the ones already in your closet. Avoid shopping for clothes when you already have more clothes than you'll ever wear. No amount is too small.

6.   **Establish and Support Male Mentoring Programs**

The abuser may listen to another male better than he would to a woman. There are some men who cannot receive the leadership of a woman, especially if his pastor is female. It is hard to believe in this day and time but it is still a factor in the church. My ex-husband could not give any specifics but there was a definite declaration that he did not believe in my call to preach and he could never sit under a woman as his pastor. This attitude can change for the better if handled with spiritual guidance and in an appropriate environment.

Men who consistently hear from other men what the expected roles and responsibilities of being a true head-of-household involve are likely to listen with results. Mentorships are limited within the community, especially for those churches with few male members. Nevertheless, there has to be a forum in the church for teaching and growing men into God-ordained roles. I have attended churches where the men greet and refer to one another as "man of God." I imagine that it's a term of endearment, used as a testament to recognize godly living inside and outside of the church walls.

Find those men in your congregation who actually demonstrate how to be a father and a husband according to God's Word. Encourage them to be leaders and mentors in the church's men's ministry. Invite the other men to attend (with a promise of confidentiality) and discuss with judgement the details of being a man after God's own heart. Some men truly do not understand that their abusive behavior is contrary to the Word of God and is just simply **wrong.** In some instances, an abuser is reflecting what he saw growing up in his own home. Men who as children witnessed their parents' domestic violence are twice as likely to abuse their wives, when compared to sons of nonviolent parents.[21]

7.   Security and "Men of Valor" Training

If a domestic violence suspect came to your church doors with an intent to injure or kill a person attending your next Sunday service, would your security personnel know what to do? Would they know where to

---

[21] http://domesticviolencestatistics.org/domestic-violence-statistics/ (10/8/2015)

look on the victim's restraining order to use when prohibiting the abuser's entry? Who controls the flow of traffic through your multiple exits? Do those assigned to protect and serve the leadership as "men of valor" or adjutants know what to do when the pastor calls for a conference with a victim?

If you do not know the answer to any one of these questions, you are not prepared to handle a domestic violence incident. I am reminded of a CNN news flash during one of my domestic violence task force meetings. On September 20, 2015, we were in the middle of planning the upcoming leadership training when all of our smartphones started alerting us. Apparently, a man walked into a church service and sat down beside his girlfriend and her infant. He started shooting them within minutes. The pastor was shot while trying to subdue the shooter. According to the Selma police in this report, there may have been a dispute over child visitation and ongoing domestic violence between Minter, the shooter, and the girlfriend according to CNN. The conversation about planning a workshop for churches shifted to a higher level after the disturbing news flashed across our various phones. One of the many questions and issues we discussed dealt with the lack of church security in that sad story.

There used to be a time when churches were considered Holy ground and safe sanctuaries. No person would have dared to smoke a cigarette in the parking lot, let alone fire off a volley of gun shots into the House of Worship. Not so anymore! But in this day of falling away (apostasy), some have lost a true reverence for God and the things of God. A church is just another place for a killing ground for the abuser intent on killing, stealing, and destroying (cf. John 10:10). For such a time as this, we have to be prepared to defend ourselves even in the church and on church grounds (Esth. 4:14).

Encourage those who are having domestic violence issues to leave a copy of their restraining orders with the administrative office and security. In North Carolina, the restraining order form has a place to enter the church's name and address as "other places" where the abuser is prohibited from having contact with the victim. Please! Please! Honor the Court's order by not allowing the abuser to be in same place at the same time as the victim. This further violates the victim's trust and sense of security. If you just cannot bring yourself to excommunicate the abuser from the congregation, and he really wants to continue his membership, consider a second service attendance policy or even a transfer to a sister-church. Remember, think SAFETY FIRST!

Make sure security has a detailed protocol to follow in the event of an incident. Some law enforcement agencies within your community may even help in the developing a plan and helping with training. Of course, being able to contact the police immediately is crucial. Everyone and their grandmother has a cell phone nowadays - so should security personnel. Establish a chain of command as to who is responsible for calling for help and alerting others of the potential for conflict if an abuser drives into the church parking lot during a service.

These steps toward developing a preparedness plan should diminish the chance of violence occurring in church. Check with your church's insurance provider so as to include the risk factors of having armed security, or of allowing known abusers attend church services.

Chapter 10: Workshop Scenarios For Group Discussion

DISCLAIMER: The following DISCUSSION POINTS and CASE SCENARIOS are used when I hold workshops for local churches and their leadership. As mentioned, the scope of these discussions is limited to the laws and policies of North Carolina. For those outside of North Carolina, please consult your legal resources before implementing any type of church by-laws, policies, and procedures.

Defining Domestic Violence, Identifying Signs and Symptoms, and Appropriate Responses

Scenario #1 – Sister Martha requests a meeting with you to discuss some problems at home. During the meeting, she discloses years of verbal insults, threats, and harassment by her husband. In the early days of their marriage and before having children, Martha admits that she engaged in arguments with him. But now she's learned to hold her peace and just wait on the Lord to release her from this situation. According to Martha, Deacon John wakes up each morning hurling profanities and degrading her about almost everything. By the end of the day, this behavior escalates to threats of finally ridding himself of her and starting over with his lover, Jezebel. He never touches her during these tirades but he gets so close that she feels afraid of him. She fears it's just a matter of time before he carries out his threats. Martha, who is usually so mentally sharp and organized in her thought process, stands before you a murmuring mess of jumbled thoughts about possibly seeking psychological help. She wants you to advise her about her options including whether to stay and wait on the Lord.

Discussion Questions:

1) Has domestic violence occurred in Scenario #1? (See legal definitions)

2) What does the Bible say about whether she is abused?

3) What are some appropriate responses to Martha's disclosure?

4) What are some inappropriate responses to Martha's discloser?

Church Security, Confidentiality, Bylaws Requirement for Known Abuse, and Implementation of "Safety First" Protocol

Scenario #2 – Two months later, Sister Martha comes up to the altar for prayer. She appears thinner than normal, disheveled in her excessively layered clothing, and crying behind darkened eyewear. She doesn't say anything other than "Please pray for me" and "God will help my marriage get better," but when you reached to hug her shoulder she instinctively blocked your grasp as if to protect an injury. She adjusted her body's position to receive your hug. Suddenly, you heard a faint whimper as if she experienced discomfort or pain. After the service, you requested a brief meeting with Martha in the privacy of your office. She reluctantly came but appeared withdrawn and almost afraid to speak. You asked the question, "Martha, is John hurting you?" However, before she could answer, Deacon John knocked on your door looking for his wife and reminded her of the late-hour. As she timidly moved toward the door, Martha secretly tilted her darkened glasses just enough for you to see blackened and bruised eyes. No verbal answer was ever spoken. Deacon John promises to return for the evening service as he escorts his wife out of your office.

Discussion Questions:

1) What are the signs and symptoms of abuse in this scenario?

2) **Should** you respond to what you observed? What, if anything, **can** you do to about your observations?

3) Was this a confidential disclosure? What about when she secretly tipped her shades (eyewear) down so you could see her injuries?

4) Can you keep Deacon John from serving during the afternoon service? What about removing him from any leadership positions?

Confidentiality, Limitations of Confidentiality, Risks to Consider for the Minister and the Victim, and Bylaws for Leadership Misconduct

Scenario #3 - After the second service, you gather up enough nerve to go see about Sister Martha and to talk with Deacon John. Upon your arrival, Deacon John meets you in the driveway and there's no sign of Sister Martha. You tell him about your observations and request permission to come inside for a discussion with both of them. Deacon John tells you that it's none of your business and to leave his property. While he's talking to you about how it's a private matter, Martha sticks her head out long enough for you to see her fearful and bruised eyes. You politely request permission to at least talk to Martha, but Deacon John reminds you that he is the priest of that house as preached to him just last Sunday. Again, but now with a little more force, he demands that you leave. Before returning to your car, you tell Deacon John that you just want to help and as his pastor/church leader, you think it is only right that you take action. At this point, Deacon John has had enough of you and threatens to "kick your butt" and gets close enough to your face for you to smell the alcohol on his breath.

Discussion Questions:

1) Is there an issue of trespassing at this point since he asked you to leave?
2) Do you have grounds to call the police if you have not spoken directly to Martha?
3) Identify some of the risks for the pastor just wanting to "take action."
4) If Martha tells you later that he only hits her because he drinks too much, what is your response?
5) What should the pastor, church leader, or a helper do about Deacon John's behavior? What does your church's by-laws and covenants say about misconduct of an officer, a leader, or a member?

Protecting Youth in Unhealthy Relationships - Duty to Report Abuse of Children

Scenario #4 – You are visually shaken by this encounter with Deacon John and decide to pull yourself together at the local Starbucks before going home. You notice Abigail, Martha and John's teenaged daughter, sitting in a dark corner with an unknown male. Abigail appears nervous and looks away as you attempt to make eye-contact. After placing your order, you decide to greet Abbey and her male friend, Nabal. Immediately, Nabal introduces himself and answers every question directed to Abigail. Abigail, who is usually bubbly and a "go-getter", never lifts her head to speak. You ask to speak with her privately, but she rejects your request as she looks at Nabal's lifted eyebrow. It's clear to you that she's under his control. Rather than leave right away, you decide to stay around without making it obvious that you're watching them. Then, Nábal steps outside to take a telephone call. Quickly moving to her table, you ask Abbey if she's all right. She fearfully responds by telling you to please leave because her boyfriend is very jealous and protective of her. Now, it becomes clear to you why this "A-B" honor roll student who plans to attend the best of the HBCUs, Hampton University, once she graduates from the church's academy, has suddenly dropped to a "barely passing" student and skips classes routinely. Nábal returned and grabbed her arm.

Discussion Questions:

1) Identify Nabal's abusive characteristics? What are other signals of a possible abusive dating relationship?

2) Can either of her parents pursue a domestic violence protection and restraining order even if Abigail does not want one?

3) What impact could her living in an abusive home have on Abbey's choice of mate and the decision to stay in the relationship?

Duty to Report Child Abuse, Safety-First Protocol, and Confidentiality

Scenario #5 – You are assigned as Youth Ministry Director by Pastor James. During the church youth program's "Let's Just Talk" session on the following Wednesday, Martha and John's other two children describe a horrific incident that happened Sunday night. They said their dad was furious after Reverend Helper left the driveway. The children told of how Deacon John stood over their mother with ball-knuckled fists yelling threats and obscenities as she remained on the floor in a fetal position. The oldest, Joseph, being fed up with years of screams and the sound of his mother's body hitting furniture, decided to protect Martha by getting between them. Outraged by his son's bravery, Deacon John forcefully pushed the boy against the wall while threatening to beat him after he finished with Martha. Joseph's head still has a sore knot from the impact. Their younger daughter, Mary, observed everything and is now so traumatized that she's begging the youth minister to keep her. Neither child wants to return home nor feels like Martha can or will protect them from Deacon John. They tearfully claim that after years of seeing beatings and the resulting bruises, and hearing their mother's screams and late-night cries, it is just a matter of time before their dad turns on them. The minister comes to you with this information.

Discussion Questions:

1) Does confidentiality rules prevent you from talking about this with the pastor?
2) What is your legal duty toward the children in Scenario No. 5?
3) Should you talk with Deacon John and Martha first?
4) Are you able to keep the children in your care?

DISCLAIMER (The Fine Print **Again**): *This does not provide legal advice for any specific person or agency, as each will have different concerns and facts about the questions that could change their answer. This INFORMATION is meant only to provide general legal information and to help give FIVE-FOLD members some background on the question.*

CONFIDENTIALITY CASE SCENARIOS

1. You had prayer with a member during altar call. This person reveals that she is being abused by her boyfriend and wants you to pray that God will make a way of escape for her. After church, the member's father comes up to ask you to let him know about his daughter's prayer. He's concerned because of signs and symptoms of abuse, but he just hasn't been able to prove it. Her dad just wants her to know that she will be safe with him. Can you tell him?

   Answer: No. She has not authorized you to discuss her confidential prayer. Encourage him to talk his daughter without revealing what she disclosed to you.

2. Brother Barry just lost his job and he's in need of a temporary loan from the church benevolence fund. At home, his children have not eaten a full meal in a while and his wife wants to take the kids to her parents. He's about to lose everything. Brother Barry wants it done in a way that no one will find out because of his pride. You suggest he come to the men's prayer session on Saturday because it's a possibility that the offering can be donated to him. Brother Barry is a "no-show" for Saturday but you ask for a special offering for his family without sharing his problems. Have you violated Brother Barry's expectation of confidentiality? What if this was told to a Deacon and not to a Minister?

   Answer: Yes. Remember that his pride issues kept him from seeking help in the first place. The deacon is not an extension of you. It is still violating his expectation of confidentiality.

3. The "have you heard" grapevine has taken root in the church. At every church function it seems that someone is talking about Sister Salome's son getting arrested for possession of drugs and being a part of a gang's breaking and entering into homes initiation. Sister Salome was just at the altar last month praying for her son because she suspected his criminal behavior. Apparently, everybody already knows so you call a group of dedicated prayer warriors that evening to have corporate prayer based on what Sister Salome told you at the altar. Have you breached confidentiality even though it Sister Salome's son's problems appear to be "public knowledge" now?

Answer: Yes. Regardless of what you think has become public knowledge, you cannot talk about anything discussed with you in confidential discussions.

4. Mary has been in regular confidential pastoral counseling sessions with you. Without explanation, she stopped coming. You have not been able to reach her by phone. Her known abuser will not let you through the front door. You suspect something is wrong but cannot prove he is hiding something. As you leave, you hear screams from Mary because her abuser thinks you came to see her. If you call the police and tell them about her abusive relationship based upon your counseling sessions, have you breached your confidential relationship with Mary?

Answer: Yes, BUT the emergency situation of hearing screams morally and legally protect you. The police can make a welfare check based upon your call for emergency help. It's the same as if a neighbor called about the screams coming from an adjoining apartment. You have to do something! You can testify, if necessary, about the screams but the previous sessions may still be under seal.

IN CONCLUSION -

The purpose of this book is to open a line of communication about domestic violence in the church. Not all churches, clergy or church leaders need this manual. Prayerfully, the discussion will continue and provoke a movement of prevention rather than reactionary agendas. In no way is this manuscript considered the answer to all that ails the victim of abuse and the church leadership. But hopefully, as a resource, leadership will become more confident in providing help and victim's will become empowered to seek help.

We all have a role in stopping and preventing abuse. Not just the church, but the legal system also has to take a zero-tolerance approach in dealing with this generational issue. For example, it is shameful that some state legislatures make stealing property a felony but hitting a woman only a misdemeanor. There are judicial officials who will set extremely low secure custody bonds upon issuing an order for the abuser's arrest. As a result, the financially controlling abuser will be out before the victim can catch a cab home from the courthouse. The final example for your consideration deals with law enforcement. There are some police officers still arriving in response to a 911 plea for help only to say, "Maybe he just needs to cool off for a period."

So several parts of the community hold some responsibility in domestic violence scenarios, not just the church. The VEIL must be taken away. This manual is intended as a charge to no longer cover our faces with veils as did Moses in Exodus 34. ("When Moses had finished speaking with them, he put a veil over his face," Ex. 34:33 NASB). Domestic violence kills and steals lives for generations. As clergy, we have to speak and act as one body in Christ with a zero-tolerance policy from the pulpit to the front doors of the church. We cannot point fingers. We cannot cast stones. But we can PRAY and THEN ACT!

References and Resources

Communications between clergymen and communicants. (2015). *North Carolina General Statute Section 8-52.2.*

Farlex. (2015). *Agency Legal Definition.* Retrieved from Legal-Dictionary/The Free Dictionary.com: www.legal-dictionary.com

Jakes, T. D. (2013). *Let It Go: Forgive So you Can Be Fogiven.* New York, NY: Atria Paperback.

Lockyer, H. (n.d.). *All the Women of the Bible.* Grand Rapids, Michigan: Zondervan.

Martins, M. (n.d.). Woman with Veil. *Unraveling the Soul.* Rio de janeiro, Brazil.

Miles, R. A. (2000). *Domestic Violence: What Every Pastor Needs to Know.* Minneapolis, MN: Fortress Press.

National Crime Survey. (1995). Retrieved from United States Department of Justice.

North Carolina General Statute Chapter 50B-1 . (2015). *Domestic Violence Definition.*

Perry, N. (2015, December 6). Brown cancels Down Under Tour after visa troubles. *Associated Press. reprinted in The Daily Dispath, Henderson, NC.*

Power and Control Wheel. (n.d.). Retrieved from National Center on Domestic and Sexual Violence: www.ncdav.org

Roget's II. (1988). In *The New Thesauus, The Expanded Edition.* New York: Berkley /books.

Society, E. R. (2016). *What is Domestic Violence Against Women and Children? Cycle of Violence Model.* Retrieved from http://www.easternrefugesociety.org

State v. Andrews, 131 N.C.App 370, 507 S.E.2d 305 (North Carolina Court of Appeals 1998).

State v. Pulley, 180 N.C.App 54 (North Carolina Court of Appeals 2006).

Swagman, B. (2002). *Responding to Domestic Violence: A Resource for Church Leaders.* Grand Rapids, Michigan: CRC Publications.

The Holy Bible, KJV. (n.d.).

The Ryrie NASB Study Bible: A complete Study and Reference Tool. (1995 Update). In T. P. Charles Caldwell Ryrie, *New American Standard Bible* (pp. 1883-1884). Chicago: The Moody Bible Institute of Chicago.

United States Department of Justice. (2015). Retrieved from Office on Violence Against Women: http://www.justice.gov/ovw

Made in the USA
Middletown, DE
07 June 2021

41309458R00058